ONE HUNDRED YEARS OF SOLITUDE

Gabriel García Márquez

EDITORIAL DIRECTOR Justin Kestler
EXECUTIVE EDITOR Ben Florman
DIRECTOR OF TECHNOLOGY Tammy Hepps

SERIES EDITORS Boomie Aglietti, John Crowther, Justin Kestler
PRODUCTION Vince Janoski

WRITERS Margaret Miller, Josh Perry
EDITORS John Crowther, Benjamin Morgan, Dennis Quinio

This edition published by Spark Publishing

Spark Publishing
A Division of SparkNotes LLC
120 Fifth Avenue, 8th Floor
New York, NY 10011

Please submit all comments and questions or report errors to www.sparknotes.com/errors

Library of Congress Catalog-in-Publication Data available upon request

Printed in China

ISBN 1-58663-454-2

Introduction:
Stopping to Buy SparkNotes on a Snowy Evening

Whose words these are you *think* you know.
Your paper's due tomorrow, though;
We're glad to see you stopping here
To get some help before you go.

Lost your course? You'll find it here.
Face tests and essays without fear.
Between the words, good grades at stake:
Get great results throughout the year.

Once school bells caused your heart to quake
As teachers circled each mistake.
Use SparkNotes and no longer weep,
Ace every single test you take.

Yes, books are lovely, dark, and deep,
But only what you grasp you keep,
With hours to go before you sleep,
With hours to go before you sleep.

Contents

Context

ABRIEL GARCÍA MÁRQUEZ WAS BORN in 1928, in the small town of Aracataca, Colombia. He started his career as a journalist, first publishing his short stories and novels in the mid-1950s. When *One Hundred Years of Solitude* was published in his native Spanish in 1967, as *Cien años de soledad,* García Márquez achieved true international fame; he went on to receive the Nobel Prize for Literature in 1982. Still a prolific writer of fiction and journalism, García Márquez was perhaps the central figure in the so-called *Latin Boom,* which designates the rise in popularity of Latin-American writing in the 1960s and 1970s. *One Hundred Years of Solitude* is perhaps the most important, and the most widely read, text to emerge from that period. It is also a central and pioneering work in the movement that has become known as magical realism, which was characterized by the dreamlike and fantastic elements woven into the fabric of its fiction.

In part, the magic of García Márquez's writing is a result of his rendering the world through a child's eyes: he has said that nothing really important has happened to him since he was eight years old and that the atmosphere of his books is the atmosphere of childhood. García Márquez's native town of Aracataca is the inspiration for much of his fiction, and readers of *One Hundred Years of Solitude* may recognize many parallels between the real-life history of García Márquez's hometown and the history of the fictional town of Macondo. In both towns, foreign fruit companies brought many prosperous plantations to nearby locations at the beginning of the twentieth century. By the time of García Márquez's birth, however, Aracataca had begun a long, slow decline into poverty and obscurity, a decline mirrored by the fall of Macondo in *One Hundred Years of Solitude.*

Even as it draws from García Márquez's provincial experiences, *One Hundred Years of Solitude* also reflects political ideas that apply to Latin America as a whole. Latin America once had a thriving population of native Aztecs and Incas, but, slowly, as European explorers arrived, the native population had to adjust to the technology and capitalism that the outsiders brought with them. Similarly, Macondo begins as a very simple settlement, and money and technology become common only when people from the outside world begin to arrive. In addition to mirroring this early virginal stage of Latin America's growth, *One Hundred Years of Solitude* reflects the current political status of various Latin American countries. Just as Macondo undergoes frequent changes in government, Latin American nations, too, seem unable to produce governments that are both stable and organized. The various dictatorships that come into power throughout the course of *One Hundred Years of Solitude*, for example, mirror dictatorships that have ruled in Nicaragua, Panama, and Cuba. García Márquez's real-life political leanings are decidedly revolutionary, even communist: he is a friend of Fidel Castro. But his depictions of cruel dictatorships show that his communist sympathies do not extend to the cruel governments that Communism sometimes produces.

One Hundred Years of Solitude, then, is partly an attempt to render the reality of García Márquez's own experiences in a fictional narrative. Its importance, however, can also be traced back to the way it appeals to broader spheres of experience. *One Hundred Years of Solitude* is an extremely ambitious novel. To a certain extent, in its sketching of the histories of civil war, plantations, and labor unrest, *One Hundred Years of Solitude* tells a story about Colombian history and, even more broadly, about Latin America's struggles with colonialism and with its own emergence into modernity. García Márquez's masterpiece, however, appeals not just to Latin American experiences, but to larger questions about human nature. It is, in the end, a novel as much about specific social and historical circumstances—disguised by fiction and fantasy—as about the possibility of love and the sadness of alienation and solitude.

PLOT OVERVIEW

ONE HUNDRED YEARS OF SOLITUDE is the history of the isolated town of Macondo and of the family who founds it, the Buendías. For years, the town has no contact with the outside world, except for gypsies who occasionally visit, peddling technologies like ice and telescopes. The patriarch of the family, José Arcadio Buendía, is impulsive and inquisitive. He remains a leader who is also deeply solitary, alienating himself from other men in his obsessive investigations into mysterious matters. These character traits are inherited by his descendents throughout the novel. His older child, José Arcadio, inherits his vast physical strength and his impetuousness. His younger child, Aureliano, inherits his intense, enigmatic focus. Gradually, the village loses its innocent, solitary state when it establishes contact with other towns in the region. Civil wars begin, bringing violence and death to peaceful Macondo, which, previously, had experienced neither, and Aureliano becomes the leader of the Liberal rebels, achieving fame as Colonel Aureliano Buendía. Macondo changes from an idyllic, magical, and sheltered place to a town irrevocably connected to the outside world through the notoriety of Colonel Buendía. Macondo's governments change several times during and after the war. At one point, Arcadio, the cruelest of the Buendías, rules dictatorially and is eventually shot by a firing squad. Later, a mayor is appointed, and his reign is peaceful until another civil uprising has him killed. After his death, the civil war ends with the signing of a peace treaty.

More than a century goes by over the course of the book, and so most of the events that García Márquez describes are the major turning points in the lives of the Buendías: births, deaths, marriages, love affairs. Some of the Buendía men are wild and sexually rapacious, frequenting brothels and taking lovers. Others are quiet and solitary, preferring to shut themselves up in their rooms to make tiny golden fish or to pore over ancient manuscripts. The women, too, range from the outrageously outgoing, like Meme, who once brings home seventy-two friends from boarding school, to the prim and proper Fernanda del Carpio, who wears a special nightgown with a hole at the crotch when she consummates her marriage with her husband.

A sense of the family's destiny for greatness remains alive in its tenacious matriarch, Ursula Iguarán, and she works devotedly to keep the family together despite its differences. But for the Buendía family, as for the entire village of Macondo, the centrifugal forces of modernity are devastating. Imperialist capitalism reaches Macondo as a banana plantation moves in and exploits the land and the workers, and the Americans who own the plantation settle in their own fenced-in section of town. Eventually, angry at the inhumane way in which they are treated, the banana workers go on strike. Thousands of them are massacred by the army, which sides with the plantation owners. When the bodies have been dumped into the sea, five years of ceaseless rain begin, creating a flood that sends Macondo into its final decline. As the city, beaten down by years of violence and false progress, begins to slip away, the Buendía family, too, begins its process of final erasure, overcome by nostalgia for bygone days. The book ends almost as it began: the village is once again solitary, isolated. The few remaining Buendía family members turn in upon themselves incestuously, alienated from the outside world and doomed to a solitary ending. In the last scene of the book, the last surviving Buendía translates a set of ancient prophecies and finds that all has been predicted: that the village and its inhabitants have merely been living out a preordained cycle, incorporating great beauty and great, tragic sadness.

CHARACTER LIST

A NOTE ABOUT THE NAMES

One of the themes of *One Hundred Years of Solitude* is the way history repeats itself in cycles. In this novel, each generation is condemned to repeat the mistakes—and to celebrate the triumphs—of the previous generation. To dramatize this point, García Márquez has given his protagonists, the Buendía family members, a very limited selection of names. *One Hundred Years of Solitude* spans six generations, and in each generation, the men of the Buendía line are named José Arcadio or Aureliano and the women are named Úrsula, Amaranta, or Remedios. Telling the difference between people who have the same name can sometimes be difficult. To a certain extent, this is to be expected: after all, García Márquez's point is precisely that human nature does not really change, that the Buendía family is locked into a cycle of repetitions. To preserve a clear notion of the plot progression, however, it is important to pay attention to the full names of the protagonists, which often contain slight distinguishing variations. José Arcadio Buendía, for instance, is a very different character than his son, José Arcadio: although it is true that José Arcadio's last name is also "Buendía," he is never referred to, either by García Márquez or in this SparkNote, as anything but "José Arcadio." And so on.

In cases where two characters are referred to by the *exact* same name (for instance, Aureliano Segundo's son is also known as "José Arcadio"), we have added a roman numeral to the character's name for the sake of clarity, even though that roman numeral does not appear in García Márquez's book: the second José Arcadio, then, appears as José Arcadio (II). Keep in mind that José Arcadio (II) is not the son of the first José Arcadio; he is merely the second José Arcadio in the book.

THE BUENDÍA FAMILY

FIRST GENERATION

José Arcadio Buendía The patriarch of the Buendía clan, José Arcadio Buendía is Macondo's founder and its most charismatic citizen. He is a man of great strength and curiosity. Impulsively, he embarks on mad pursuits of esoteric and practical knowledge, and it is his solitary and obsessive quest for knowledge that drives him mad at the end of his life; he spends many years, in the end, tied to a tree in the Buendía backyard, speaking Latin that only the priest understands. José Arcadio Buendía is married to Úrsula Iguarán and the father of José Arcadio, Colonel Aureliano Buendía, and Amaranta.

Úrsula Iguarán The tenacious matriarch of the Buendía clan, Úrsula lives to be well over a hundred years old, continuing with her hard-headed common sense to try and preserve the family. Every now and then, when things get particularly run-down, Úrsula revitalizes the family both physically and emotionally, repairing the Buendía house and breathing new life into the family. She is the wife of José Arcadio Buendía and the mother of José Arcadio, Colonel Aureliano Buendía, and Amaranta.

SECOND GENERATION

Amaranta   The daughter of Úrsula Iguarán and José Arcadio Buendía, Amaranta dies an embittered and lonely virgin. She bears deep jealousy and hatred for Rebeca, whom, she believes, stole Pietro Crespi from her. In many ways her life is characterized by a fear of men; when Pietro Crespi finally falls in love with her, she rejects him, and he kills himself. As penance, she gives herself a bad burn on the hand and wears a black bandage over it for the rest of her life. When she is much older, she finds real love with Colonel Gerineldo Márquez, but she spurns him because of her ancient fear and bitterness. She is also the object of the unconsummated incestuous passion of Aureliano José, whom she helped to raise. Amaranta is the sister of Colonel Aureliano Buendía and José Arcadio.

Colonel Aureliano Buendía The second son of José Arcadio Buendía and Úrsula Iguarán. Aureliano grows up solitary and enigmatic, with a strange capacity for extrasensory perception. Outraged by the corruption of the Conservative government, he joins the Liberal rebellion and becomes Colonel Aureliano Buendía, the rebel commander. After years of fighting, he loses his capacity for memory and deep emotion, signs a peace accord, and withdraws into his workshop, a lonely and hardened man. He is the widower of Remedios Moscote and the father, with Pilar Ternera, of Aureliano José, and of seventeen sons—each named Aureliano—by seventeen different women.

Remedios Moscote The child-bride of Colonel Aureliano Buendía, Remedios Moscote brings joy to the Buendía household for a short while before she dies suddenly, possibly of a miscarriage.

José Arcadio The first son of Úrsula Iguarán and José Arcadio Buendía, from whom he inherits his amazing strength and his impulsive drive. After running off in pursuit of a gypsy girl, José Arcadio returns a savage brute of a man and marries Rebeca, the orphan adopted by the Buendías. He is the father, with Pilar Ternera, of Arcadio, and brother to Colonel Aureliano Buendía and Amaranta.

Rebeca The earth-eating orphan girl who mysteriously arrives at the Buendía doorstep. Rebeca is adopted by the Buendí family. Rebeca infects the town with an insomnia that causes loss of memory. Rebeca seems to orphan herself from society and the Buendía family when, after her husband José Arcadio's death, she becomes a hermit, never seen outside her dilapidated home.

THIRD GENERATION

Aureliano José The son of Colonel Aureliano Buendía and Pilar Ternera. Aureliano José becomes obsessed with his aunt, Amaranta, and joins his father's army when she ends the affair. He deserts the army to return to her, however, but she rejects him, horrified. He is killed by Conservative soldiers.

Arcadio The son of José Arcadio and Pilar Ternera. Arcadio, seemingly a gentle boy, becomes schoolmaster of the town. When Colonel Aureliano Buendía places him in charge of Macondo during the uprising, however, Arcadio proves a vicious dictator who is obsessed with order. He is killed when the conservatives retake the village. Arcadio marries Santa Sofía de la Piedad and is the father of Remedios the Beauty, Aureliano Segundo, and José Arcadio Segundo.

Santa Sofía de la Piedad The quiet woman, almost invisible in this novel, who marries Arcadio and continues to live in the Buendía house for many years after his death, impassively tending to the family. She is the mother of Remedios the Beauty, Aureliano Segundo, and José Arcadio Segundo. She does not quite seem to exist in the real world, and when she grows old and tired, she simply walks out of the house, never to be heard from again.

FOURTH GENERATION

Remedios the Beauty The daughter of Santa Sofía de la Piedad and Arcadio, Remedios the Beauty becomes the most beautiful woman in the world: desire for her drives men to their deaths. Not comprehending her power over men, she remains innocent and childlike. One day, she floats to heaven, leaving Macondo and the novel abruptly.

José Arcadio Segundo The son of Arcadio and Santa Sofía de la Piedad, José Arcadio Segundo may have been switched at birth with his twin brother, Aureliano Segundo. Appalled by witnessing an execution at an early age,

José Arcadio Segundo becomes thin, bony, solitary, and increasingly scholarly, like his great-uncle Colonel Aureliano Buendía. A cockfighter and a drifter, he finds purpose in leading the strikers against the banana company. He is the lone survivor of the massacre of the strikers, and when he finds that nobody believes the massacre occurred, he secludes himself in Melquíades' old study, trying to decipher the old prophecies and preserving the memory of the massacre.

Aureliano Segundo The son of Arcadio and Santa Sofía de la Piedad, Aureliano Segundo may have been switched at birth with his twin brother, José Arcadio Segundo. Despite an early interest in solitary study—characteristic of his great-uncle, Colonel Aureliano Buendía—Aureliano Segundo begins to show all the characteristics of the family's José Arcadios: he is immense, boisterous, impulsive, and hedonistic. Although he loves the concubine Petra Cotes, he is married to the cold beauty Fernanda del Carpio, with whom he has three children: Meme, José Arcadio (II) and Amaranta Úrsula.

Fernanda del Carpio The wife of Aureliano Segundo and the mother of Meme, José Arcadio (II), and Amaranta Úrsula. Fernanda del Carpio was raised by a family of impoverished aristocrats; she is very haughty and very religious. Her hedonistic husband does not love her and maintains his relationship with his concubine, Petra Cotes. Fernanda del Carpio, meanwhile, tries unsuccessfully to impress her sterile religion and aristocratic manners on the Buendía house.

FIFTH GENERATION

José Arcadio (II) The eldest child of Aureliano Segundo and Fernanda del Carpio, Úrsula decides that José Arcadio (II) is supposed to become the Pope, but he in fact slides into dissolution and solitude. On his return from his unsuccessful trip to seminary in Italy, José Arcadio (II) leads a life of debauchery with local adolescents who eventually murder him and steal his money.

Amaranta Úrsula The daughter of Aureliano Segundo and Fernanda del Carpio, Amaranta Úrsula returns from her trip to Europe with a Belgian husband, Gaston. She wants to revitalize Macondo and the Buendía household, but it is too late: both are headed for inevitable ruin. She falls in love with her nephew, Aureliano (II), and gives birth to his child, whom they also name Aureliano (III) and who proves the last in the Buendía line. Born of incest, he has the tail of a pig. Amaranta dies in childbirth.

Gaston The Belgian husband of Amaranta Úrsula, Gaston is loving and cultured but feels isolated in the now-desolate Macondo. He travels to Belgium to start an airmail company, and, when he hears of the relationship between his wife and Aureliano (II), he never returns.

Meme The daughter of Fernanda del Carpio and Aureliano Segundo, Meme's real name is Renata Remedios. She feigns studiousness and docility to please her mother, but she is actually a hedonist like her father. When her mother discovers her illicit affair with Mauricio Babilonia, she posts a guard in front of the house; the guard ends up shooting Mauricio. He ends up paralyzed, and Meme is imprisoned in a convent where she spends the rest of her life. The product of her affair with Babilonia is Aureliano (II).

SIXTH GENERATION
Aureliano (II) The illegitimate son of Meme and Mauricio Babilonia, Aureliano (II) is concealed by his scandalized grandmother, Fernanda del Carpio. He grows up a hermit in the Buendía household, only gradually acclimating himself to society. Aureliano (II) becomes a scholar, and it is he who eventually deciphers the prophecies of Melquíades. With his aunt, Amaranta Úrsula, he fathers the last in the Buendía line, the baby Aureliano (III), who dies soon after birth.

Characters who are not members of the Buendía Family

Melquíades The gypsy who brings technological marvels to Macondo and befriends the Buendía clan. Melquíades is the first person to die in Macondo. Melquíades serves as José Arcadio Buendía's guide in his quest for knowledge and, even after dying, returns to guide other generations of Buendías. Melquíades' mysterious and undecipherable prophecies, which torment generations of Buendías, are finally translated by Aureliano (II) at the end of the novel—they contain the entire history of Macondo, foretold.

Pilar Ternera A local whore and madam. With José Arcadio, Pilar is the mother of Arcadio; with Colonel Aureliano Buendía, she is the mother of Aureliano José. She is also a fortune-teller whose quiet wisdom helps guide the Buendía family. She survives until the very last days of Macondo.

Petra Cotes Aureliano Segundo's concubine. Petra Cotes and Aureliano Segundo become extremely rich—their own love seems to inspire their animals to procreate unnaturally quickly. Even after the poverty caused by the flood, she stays with Aureliano Segundo; their deepened love is one of the purest emotions in the novel.

Mauricio Babilonia The sallow, solemn lover of Meme. Fernanda del Carpio disapproves of their affair, and she sets up a guard who shoots Mauricio Babilonia when he attempts to climb into the house for a tryst with Meme. As a result, Mauricio lives the rest of his life completely paralyzed. He fathers Meme's child, Aureliano (II).

Pietro Crespi The gentle, delicate Italian musician who is loved by both Amaranta and Rebeca. Rebeca, however, chooses to marry the more manly José Arcadio. After Amaranta leads on Pietro and rejects him, Pietro commits suicide.

Colonel Gerineldo Márquez The comrade-in-arms of Colonel Aureliano Buendía. Colonel Gerineldo is the first to become tired of the civil war. He falls in love with Amaranta, who spurns him.

Don Apolinar Moscote Father of Remedios Moscote and government-appointed magistrate of Macondo. Don Apolinar Moscote is a Conservative and helps rig the election so that his party will win. His dishonesty is partly why Colonel Aureliano Buendía first joins the Liberals.

ANALYSIS OF MAJOR CHARACTERS

JOSÉ ARCADIO BUENDÍA

The founder and patriarch of Macondo, José Arcadio Buendía represents both great leadership and the innocence of the ancient world. He is a natural explorer, setting off into the wilderness first to found Macondo and then to find a route between Macondo and the outside world. In this tale of creation he is the Adam figure, whose quest for knowledge, mirrored in the intellectual pursuits of his descendants, eventually results in his family's loss of innocence. José Arcadio Buendía pushes his family forward into modernity, preferring the confines of his laboratory to the sight of a real flying carpet that the gypsies have brought. By turning his back on this ancient magic in favor of his more modern scientific ideas, he hastens the end of Macondo's Eden-like state.

For José Arcadio Buendía, however, madness comes sooner than disillusionment. Immediately after he thinks he has discovered a means to create perpetual motion—a physical impossibility—he goes insane, convinced that the same day is repeating itself over and over again. In a sense, his purported discovery of perpetual motion achieves a kind of total knowledge that may be too deep for the human mind to withstand. Perpetual motion could only exist in a world without time, which, for José Arcadio Buendía, is what the world becomes and, in a sense, is what time throughout the novel becomes: past, present and future often overlap. This overlapping of time allows José Arcadio Buendía to appear to his descendants in the form of a ghost, so that his presence will always be felt in Macondo.

COLONEL AURELIANO BUENDÍA

Colonel Aureliano Buendía is *One Hundred Years of Solitude*'s greatest soldier figure, leading the Liberal army throughout the civil war. At the same time, however, he is the novel's greatest artist figure: a poet, an accomplished silversmith, and the creator of hundreds of finely crafted golden fishes. Aureliano's (I) inability to experience deep emotion contributes to his great battle poise and artistic focus, yet Márquez's depiction of the Colonel melting away his hard work and starting all over again signals that this poise and focus is not worth its price.

Aureliano (I) is never truly touched by anything or anyone. His child bride, Remedios Moscote, seems at first to have a real effect on him. When she dies, however, he discovers that his sorrow is not as profound as he had expected. During the war, he becomes even more hardened to emotion, and, eventually, his memory and all his feelings are worn away. He has all of his poems burned, and, by the end of his life, he has stopped making new golden fish. Instead, he makes twenty-five and then melts them down, using the metal for the next batch. In this way, he lives solely in the present, acknowledging that time moves in cycles and that the present is all that exists for a man like him, with no memories.

Colonel Aureliano Buendía's attempted suicide shows us how deep his despair is when he realizes that civil war is futile and that pride is the only thing that keeps the two sides fighting. His disillusionment is a moving commentary on the despair that arises from futility but, also, on the futility that arises from despair.

ÚRSULA IGUARÁN

Of all the characters in the novel, Úrsula Iguarán lives the longest and sees the most new generations born. She outlives all three of her children. Unlike most of her relatives, Úrsula is untroubled by great spiritual anxiety; in this sense, she is probably the strongest person ever to live in Macondo. She takes in Rebeca, the child of strangers, and raises her as her own daughter; she welcomes dozens of passing strangers to her table; she tries to keep the house from falling apart. Úrsula's task is not easy, since all of her descendants become embroiled in wars and scandals that would cause any weaker family to dissolve. With Úrsula as their mainstay, however, the Buendías are irrevocably linked, for better or for worse. To keep the family together, Úrsula sometimes is quite harsh; for example, she kicks José Arcadio and Rebeca out of the house when they elope. This decision is partly a result of her unyielding fear of incest. Even though Rebeca and José Arcadio are not technically related, Úrsula is terrified that even a remotely incestuous action or relation will result in someone in the family having a baby with the tail of a pig. Her own marriage to José Arcadio Buendía is incestuous because

they are cousins, and she constantly examines her children's behavior for flaws, frequently saying, "[i]t's worse than if he had been born with the tail of a pig." Because of her fear of incest, Úrsula is a contradictory character: she binds the family together, but is terrified that incest, the extreme of family bonding, will bring disaster to the Buendía house.

Aureliano (II)

Aureliano (II) is the purest example in *One Hundred Years of Solitude* of the solitary, destructive Buendía thirst for knowledge. He is utterly isolated by his grandmother, Fernanda del Carpio, because she is ashamed that he was born out of wedlock. He never even leaves the house until he is fully grown. As he lives in solitude, however, he acquires a store of knowledge almost magical in scope. He knows far more than he could have read in his family's books and seems to have miraculously accessed an enormous store of universal knowledge. After having an incestuous relationship with his aunt, Amaranta Úrsula, Aureliano (II) watches the last of the Buendía line (their son, born with the tail of a pig) being eaten by ants. He finally translates the prophecies of the old gypsy, Melquíades, which foretell both the act of translation and the destruction of Macondo that occurs as he reads. Aureliano (II) is therefore Macondo's prophet of doom, destroying the town with an act of reading and translation that is similar to our reading of *One Hundred Years of Solitude*.

THEMES, MOTIFS & SYMBOLS

THEMES

Themes are the fundamental and often universal ideas explored in a literary work.

THE SUBJECTIVITY OF EXPERIENCED REALITY

Although the realism and the magic that *One Hundred Years of Solitude* includes seem at first to be opposites, they are, in fact, perfectly reconcilable. Both are necessary in order to convey Márquez's particular conception of the world. Márquez's novel reflects reality not as it is experienced by one observer, but as it is individually experienced by those with different backgrounds. These multiple perspectives are especially appropriate to the unique reality of Latin America—caught between modernity and pre-industrialization; torn by civil war, and ravaged by imperialism—where the experiences of people vary much more than they might in a more homogenous society. Magical realism conveys a reality that incorporates the magic that superstition and religion infuse into the world.

This novel treats biblical narratives and native Latin American mythology as historically credible. This approach may stem from the sense, shared by some Latin American authors, that important and powerful strains of magic running through ordinary lives fall victim to the Western emphasis on logic and reason. If García Márquez seems to confuse reality and fiction, it is only because, from some perspectives, fiction may be truer than reality, and vice versa. For instance, in places like Márquez's hometown, which witnessed a massacre much like that of the workers in Macondo, unthinkable horrors may be a common sight. Real life, then, begins to seem like a fantasy that is both terrifying and fascinating, and Márquez's novel is an attempt to recreate and to capture that sense of real life.

THE INSEPARABILITY OF PAST, PRESENT, AND FUTURE

From the names that return generation after generation to the repetition of personalities and events, time in *One Hundred Years of Sol-*

itude refuses to divide neatly into past, present, and future. Úrsula Iguarán is always the first to notice that time in Macondo is not finite, but, rather, moves forward over and over again. Sometimes, this simultaneity of time leads to amnesia, when people cannot see the past any more than they can see the future. Other times the future becomes as easy to recall as the past. The prophecies of Melquíades prove that events in time are continuous: from the beginning of the novel, the old gypsy was able to see its end, as if the various events were all occurring at once. Similarly, the presence of the ghosts of Melquíades and José Arcadio Buendía shows that the past in which those men lived has become one with the present.

The Power of Reading and of Language

Although language is in an unripe, Garden-of-Eden state at the beginning of *One Hundred Years of Solitude,* when most things in the newborn world are still unnamed, its function quickly becomes more complex. Various languages fill the novel, including the Guajiro language that the children learn, the multilingual tattoos that cover José Arcadio's body, the Latin spoken by José Arcadio Buendía, and the final Sanskrit translation of Melquíades's prophecies. In fact, this final act of translation can be seen as the most significant act in the book, since it seems to be the one that makes the book's existence possible and gives life to the characters and story within.

As García Márquez makes reading the final apocalyptic force that destroys Macondo and calls attention to his own task as a writer, he also reminds us that our reading provides the fundamental first breath to every action that takes place in *One Hundred Years of Solitude.* While the novel can be thought of as something with one clear, predetermined meaning, García Márquez asks his reader to acknowledge the fact that every act of reading is also an interpretation, and that such interpretations can have weighty consequences. Aureliano (II), then, does not just take the manuscripts' meanings for granted, but, in addition, he must also translate and interpret them and ultimately precipitate the destruction of the town.

Motifs

Motifs are recurring structures, contrasts, or literary devices that can help to develop and inform the text's major themes.

Memory and Forgetfulness

While the characters in *One Hundred Years of Solitude* consider total forgetfulness a danger, they, ironically, also seem to consider memory a burden. About half of the novel's characters speak of the weight of having too many memories while the rest seem to be amnesiacs. Rebeca's overabundance of memory causes her to lock herself in her house after her husband's death, and to live there with the memory of friends rather than the presence of people. For her, the nostalgia of better days gone by prevents her from existing in a changing world. The opposite of her character can be found in Colonel Aureliano Buendía, who has almost no memories at all. He lives in an endlessly repeating present, melting down and then recreating his collection of little gold fishes. Nostalgia and amnesia are the dual diseases of the Buendía clan, one tying its victims to the past, the other trapping them in the present. Thus afflicted, the Buendías are doomed to repeat the same cycles until they consume themselves, and they are never able to move into the future.

The Bible

One Hundred Years of Solitude draws on many of the basic narratives of the Bible, and its characters can be seen as allegorical of some major biblical figures. The novel recounts the creation of Macondo and its earliest Edenic days of innocence, and continues until its apocalyptic end, with a cleansing flood in between. We can see José Arcadio Buendía's downfall—his loss of sanity—as a result of his quest for knowledge. He and his wife, Ursula Iguarán, represent the biblical Adam and Eve, who were exiled from Eden after eating from the Tree of Knowledge. The entire novel functions as a metaphor for human history and an extended commentary on human nature. On the one hand, their story, taken literally as applying to the fictional Buendías, evokes immense pathos. But as representatives of the human race, the Buendías personify solitude and inevitable tragedy, together with the elusive possibility of happiness, as chronicled by the Bible.

The Gypsies

Gypsies are present in *One Hundred Years of Solitude* primarily to act as links. They function to offer transitions from contrasting or unrelated events and characters. Every few years, especially in the early days of Macondo, a pack of wandering gypsies arrives, turning the town into something like a carnival and displaying the wares that they have brought with them. Before Macondo has a road to civilization, they are the town's only contact with the outside world. They bring both technology—inventions that Melquíades displays—and magic—magic carpets and other wonders. Gypsies, then, serve as versatile literary devices that also blur the line between fantasy and reality, especially when they connect Macondo and the outside world, magic and science, and even the past and present.

SYMBOLS

Symbols are objects, characters, figures, or colors used to represent abstract ideas or concepts.

LITTLE GOLD FISHES

The meaning of the thousands of little gold fishes that Colonel Aureliano Buendía makes shifts over time. At first, these fishes represent Aureliano's artistic nature and, by extension, the artistic nature of all the Aurelianos. Soon, however, they acquire a greater significance, marking the ways in which Aureliano has affected the world. His seventeen sons, for example, are each given a little gold fish, and, in this case, the fishes represent Aureliano's effect on the world through his sons. In another instance, they are used as passkeys when messengers for the Liberals use them to prove their allegiance. Many years later, however, the fishes become collector's items, merely relics of a once-great leader. This attitude disgusts Aureliano because he recognizes that people are using him as a figurehead, a mythological hero that represents whatever they want it to represent. When he begins to understand that the little gold fishes no longer are symbolic of him personally, but instead of a mistaken ideal, he stops making new fishes and starts to melt down the old ones again and again.

THE RAILROAD

The railroad represents the arrival of the modern world in Macondo. This devastating turn leads to the development of a banana plantation and the ensuing massacre of three thousand workers. The railroad also represents the period when Macondo is connected most closely with the outside world. After the banana plantations close down, the railroad falls into disrepair and the train ceases even to stop in Macondo any more. The advent of the railroad is a turning point. Before it comes, Macondo grows bigger and thrives; afterward, Macondo quickly disintegrates, folding back into isolation and eventually expiring.

The English Encyclopedia

At first, the English encyclopedia that Meme receives from her American friend is a symbol for the way the American plantation owners are taking over Macondo. When Meme, a descendant of the town's founders, begins to learn English, the foreigners' encroachment on Macondo's culture becomes obvious. The concrete threat posed by the encyclopedia is later lessened when Aureliano Segundo uses it to tell his children stories. Because he does not speak English, Aureliano Segundo makes up stories to go with the pictures. By creating the possibility for multiple interpretations of the text, he unwittingly diffuses the encyclopedia's danger.

The Golden Chamber Pot

The golden chamber pot that Fernanda del Carpio brings to Macondo from her home is, for her, a marker of her lofty status; she believes that she was destined to be a queen. But while the gold of the chamber pot is associated with royalty, the function of the chamber pot is, of course, associated with defecation: a sign of the real value of Fernanda's snooty condescension. Later, when José Arcadio (II) tries to sell the chamber pot, he finds that it is not really solid gold, but, rather, gold-plated. Again, this revelation represents the hollowness of Fernanda's pride and the flimsiness of cheap cover-ups.

SYMBOLS

SUMMARY & ANALYSIS

CHAPTERS 1–2

SUMMARY: CHAPTER 1

> *At that time Macondo was a village of twenty adobe houses . . . the world was so recent that many things lacked names. . . .* (See QUOTATIONS, p. 55)

One Hundred Years of Solitude begins as a flashback, with Colonel Aureliano Buendía recollecting the years immediately following the founding of Macondo, when a band of gypsies frequently bring technological marvels to the dreamy, isolated village. José Arcadio Buendía, the insatiably curious founder of the town, is obsessed with these magical implements. Using supplies given to him by Melquíades, the leader of the gypsies, he immerses himself in scientific study, to the frustration of his more practical wife, Úrsula Iguarán. Eventually, with Melquíades's prodding, José Arcadio Buendía begins to explore alchemy, the pseudo-science of making gold out of other metals. He is driven by a desire for progress and by an intense search for knowledge that forces him into solitude. Increasingly, he withdraws from human contact, becoming unkempt, antisocial, and interested only in his pursuit of knowledge. But José Arcadio Buendía is not always a solitary scientist. On the contrary, he is the leader who oversaw the building of the village of Macondo, an idyllic place dedicated to hard work and order, filled with young people, and as yet, unvisited by death.

In his quest for knowledge and progress, José Arcadio Buendía's obsession shifts to a desire to establish contact with civilization. He leads an expedition to the north, since he knows there is only swamp to the west and south and mountains to the east. But he then decides that Macondo is surrounded by water and inaccessible to the rest of the world. When he plans to move Macondo to another, more accessible place, however, he is stopped by his wife, who refuses to leave. Thwarted, he turns his attention, finally, to his children: José Arcadio, who has inherited his father's great strength, and Aureliano (later known as Colonel Aureliano Buendía), who seems, even as a child, enigmatic and withdrawn. When the gypsies return, they bring word that Melquíades is dead. Despite his sadness at the news, José Arcadio Buendía does not lose interest in new technology and marvels: when the gypsies show him ice, the patriarch of Macondo proclaims it the greatest invention in the world.

SUMMARY: CHAPTER 2

In telling the story of Macondo's founding, the book now moves backward in time. The cousins José Arcadio Buendía and Úrsula Iguarán are born in a small village, the great-grandchildren of those surviving Sir Francis Drake's attack on Riohacha. Úrsula is afraid to consummate their marriage, as children of incest were said to have terrible genetic defects. There was precedent for this: two of their relatives gave birth to a child with a pig's tail. But as time passes after their marriage, and Ursula continues to refuse to have sex out of fear of the genetic deformity of their child, the people of the village begin to mock José Arcadio Buendía. When a rival, Prudencio Aguilar, implies that Buendía is impotent, Buendía kills him. Haunted by guilt and the specter of Aguilar, José Arcadio Buendía decides to leave his home. After many months of wandering, they establish the village of Macondo.

On seeing the ice of the gypsies, José Arcadio Buendía remembers his dream of Macondo as a city built with mirror-walls, which he interprets to mean ice. He immerses himself again in his scientific study, this time accompanied by his son Aureliano. Meanwhile, the older son, José Arcadio—still a teenager—is seduced by a local woman, Pilar Ternera, who is attracted to him because of the huge size of his penis. Eventually, he impregnates her. Before their child can be born, however, he meets a young gypsy girl and falls madly in love with her. When the gypsies leave town, José Arcadio joins them. Grief-stricken at the loss of her eldest son, Úrsula tries to follow the gypsies, leaving behind her newborn girl, Amaranta. Five months later, Úrsula returns, having discovered the simple, two-day journey through the swamp that connects Macondo with civilization.

ANALYSIS: CHAPTERS 1–2

One Hundred Years of Solitude does not adopt a straightforward approach to telling its version of history. The progression of time from the town's founding to its demise, from the origins of the Buendía clan to their destruction, provides a rough structure for the novel. But García Márquez does not necessarily tell events in the order that they happen. Rather, flitting forward and backward in time, García Márquez creates the mythic feel and informality of a meandering oral history. Although the first extended episode of the novel tells of the gypsies who come to Macondo bearing technological innovations that seem miraculous to the citizens of the isolated village, the first sentence of the novel refers to an episode far in the future, the planned execution of Colonel Aureliano Buendía. The story of the gypsies, leading up to the moment when José Arcadio Buendía sees ice for the first time, is cast as Colonel Aureliano Buendía's recollection, and so, immediately in the novel, there is a chronological disjunction.

This feeling of befuddled time is compounded by the fact that, at first, we are not sure of *One Hundred Years of Solitude*'s historical setting. At the founding of Macondo, "the world was so recent that many things lacked names," but we also learn that Ursula's great-grandmother was alive when Sir Francis Drake attacked Riohacha, an actual event that took place in 1568. In real life, this perception of time would be impossible. Obviously Sir Francis Drake lived long after the world grew old enough for every object to have a name. Critic Regina Janes points out that these two occurrences are not meant to be an accurate picture of historical events. Instead, the disjunction between them allows García Márquez to disorient us, getting us thoroughly lost in the murky historical swamp in which he has placed us.

This strangely indefinite chronological framework blurs the distinctions between memory, history, and fiction. The arrival of the gypsies in town is framed as Colonel Aureliano Buendía's memory rather than as an authoritative reframing of history. As a memory, it assumes subjective and dreamlike qualities that are supposed to be absent from textbook history. This is a narrative strategy that is evident throughout the novel—memory is given the same authority as history, and history is subject to the same emotional colorings and flights of fancy as memory. When, much later in the novel, the inhabitants of the town forget about the massacre of the banana workers, their amnesia constitutes an actual erasing of history. In *One Hundred Years of Solitude*, reality assumes the qualities of human fantasy and memory, and time itself is subject to the same distortions. People in this novel live for impossibly long periods of time, and rain descends for years without stopping; on the other hand, years sometimes pass by without mention or notice from the narrator. The extreme subjectivity of experienced reality is one of the themes of this novel. It is the human tendency toward the fantastic and the absurd that shapes our version of reality: magical realism, then, merely captures a version of reality colored by myth and memory, by human fantasy, and by our own subjectivity.

While we observe that the novel begins with a historical disjunction, however, it is important to note that *One Hundred Years of Solitude* is deliberately structured to trace a very definite narrative, one of epic—or perhaps biblical—proportions. The novel is indeed, as the critic Harold Bloom has observed, the Bible of Macondo, and, again, at the very beginning of the novel, just as in the Bible, many things have yet to be named. *One Hundred Years of Solitude* can be seen as a parable for the human quest for knowledge, expressed through the struggles of José Arcadio Buendía—the archetypal man—and his descendents. In the Bible, Adam's job is to name the animals, exercising his power over them and cataloguing them to conform to his vision of the world. In establishing Macondo, José Arcadio Buendía does the same thing. Adam and Eve were expelled from Eden for eating from the Tree of Knowledge, and this novel conveys the same cautionary tale. José Arcadio Buendía's relentless pursuit of knowledge, arguably, drives him to foolishness and eventual insanity. It should not be forgotten that, in his madness, he is tied to a tree that functions as a clear symbol for the Tree of Knowledge, whose fruit tempted Adam and Eve to their original fall.

García Márquez's style of writing is commonly referred to as magical realism, which describes, among other things, the way historical events are colored by subjectivity and memory is given the same weight as history. One easily identifiable trait of magical realism is the way in which mundane, everyday things are mingled with extraordinarily wonderful, or even supernatural, things. In Chapter 2, as José Arcadio is seduced by Pilar Ternera, we learn that "he could no longer resist the glacial rumbling of his kidneys and the air of his intestines, and the bewildered anxiety to flee and at the same time stay forever in that exasperated silence and that fearful solitude." Here, García Márquez describes very specific physical events side by side with huge, abstract emotions. This is typical of magical realism: just as the distinctions between different times are muddled up, the distinction between the real and the magical, or between the ordinary and the sublime, become confused.

CHAPTERS 3–4

SUMMARY: CHAPTER 3

As a result of Úrsula Iguarán's discovery of a route connecting Macondo with civilization, the village begins to change. The village grows along with the Buendía family, with José Arcadio Buendía playing a key role in the expansion of both. Pilar Ternera gives birth to the son of the missing José Arcadio. The boy is named Arcadio. Joining the family, too, is an orphan girl, Rebeca, who arrives mysteriously one day and whose origin is unclear. Nevertheless, the Buendías raise her as one of their own children, first conquering her self-destructive habits of eating dirt and whitewash. Rebeca, it soon becomes evident, is afflicted with an insomnia that also causes memory loss. Eventually, the entire town becomes infected with insomnia and the associated amnesia. To facilitate memory, the inhabitants of the town begin to label everything; First they put up a giant sign to remind themselves that GOD EXISTS, and then dread the day when the labels will have no meaning because the residents will have forgotten how to read. Pilar Ternera, who tells fortunes on a deck of cards, now uses the cards to tell the past as well. The insomnia is only cured when, unexpectedly, Melquíades the gypsy returns to town bearing an antidote. Melquíades, who, it seems, has returned from the dead, brings with him a technology never before seen in Macondo, the daguerreotype; José Arcadio Buendía sets to work trying to make a daguerreotype of God, to prove His existence. Aureliano, José Arcadio Buendía's second son, has become a master silversmith. He spends his days shut up in the laboratory that he shares with Melquíades, each of them obsessively absorbed with their strange pursuits. Now mature, Aureliano remains solitary and aloof, apparently uninterested in women.

As the family and village expand, Ursula vastly expands the Buendía house. The town magistrate, a representative of the central government newly arrived in the formerly autonomous Macondo, attempts to dictate the color their house will be painted. José Arcadio Buendía drives the magistrate, Don Apolinar Moscote, out of town, and when Moscote returns—accompanied by his family and several soldiers—Buendía forces him to forfeit much of his authority over the village. Despite his father's enmity toward the magistrate, however, Aureliano falls in love with the magistrate's youngest daughter, Remedios Moscote.

SUMMARY: CHAPTER 4

Lonely and despairing, Aureliano sleeps with Pilar Ternera, the same woman whom his older brother had impregnated, and she helps Aureliano in his campaign to marry Remedios. While Aureliano is pining over the impossibly young Remedios, the Buendía family's two girls—Amaranta and the adoptee Rebeca—both fall in love with a stranger, Pietro Crespi, who has come to Macondo to install a pianola in the Buendía house. They make themselves sick with love: Rebeca goes back to eating earth and whitewash, and Crespi decides he wants to marry her. The marriages—of Rebeca to Crespi and Aureliano to Remedios—are arranged, even though Amaranta, wildly jealous of Rebeca, vows to stop her marriage.

When the gypsy Melquíades slowly passes away, he is the first person to die in Macondo. After his mourning period is over, a semblance of happiness descends on the house: Pietro Crespi and Rebeca are in love, courting, and Aureliano is becoming closer to his future bride, Remedios. Even the news that Pilar Ternera is pregnant with his child does not bother Aureliano. But the happiness does not last. Amaranta's threat to destroy Rebeca's wedding deeply troubles Rebeca. José Arcadio Buendía, exhausted by his endless research into the unknown, slips into insanity. He has visions of the man he killed early in his life and is wracked with sorrow over the solitude of death. He becomes convinced that the same day is repeating itself over and over again. He begins to rage, tearing up the house, and it takes twenty men to drag him out and tie him to a tree in the backyard, where he remains until the end of his life, many years later.

ANALYSIS: CHAPTERS 3–4

It might be said that Macondo's evolution is a parable, evocative of the typical arc of human societal progress, and that the village is a microcosm for all of human civilization. In this section, the technological and social changes that accompany modernization cause the society to become more cosmopolitan, containing both greater wealth and greater social problems than Macondo did in its earlier state. Increased traffic through the town brings prosperity, but it also brings some of the horrors associated with capitalism. For example, Aureliano stumbles into a tent where a girl is being forced to sleep with many men consecutively—it will take seventy a night, for ten more years, to pay off her family's debts. The town is also changed by governmental interference that contact with the outside world allows. José Aureliano Buendía has his first encounter in this section with the civil authorities that will increasingly seize control of the town. Gradually, it is suggested, so-called progress brings loss of innocence and potential sources of conflict.

But the changes happening to the city go beyond a simple allegory of political change in world history. The conflict between José Arcadio Buendía's style of government and the regulations brought in by the magistrate reflects a political agenda that is very specific to García Márquez and Latin America. García Márquez is well known as a friend of Fidel Castro, a Communist, and revolutionary sympathizer. José Arcadio Buendía's Macondo is a utopian portrait of what an ideally communist society might be like. He has mapped out the city so that every house has equal access to water and shade, and he tells the magistrate that "in this town we do not give orders with pieces of paper." Later on, we will see that this early utopia cannot last, and Macondo will become embroiled in a revolution against a harshly regulatory government. If García Márquez appears to support an idealistically communist vision of what society *should* be like, his strong reaction against dictatorship and oppression indicates his disapproval of the oppressive tendencies that have come to be associated with the reality of communism.

One way the residents of Macondo respond to these changes is by embracing solitude more and more. In this section, the Buendías—José Arcadio Buendía and his second son, Aureliano—first begin to turn away from society, to devote themselves single-mindedly to their crafts and intellectual pursuits. José Arcadio Buendía goes insane, his mind crumbling under the pressure of his solitary musings, and he has to be tied to a tree. Symbolically, this tree is reminiscent of Eden's Tree of Knowledge, the same tree whose fruit José Arcadio Buendía has dared to eat. Aureliano's solitude seems inborn: like the village itself, he is simply happier when left alone. He seems to feel love for Remedios Moscote, but when she dies, later in the book, he feels no great sorrow. Emotions seem beyond him, as do relationships, and he is fundamentally detached from people and feelings. It will be revealed throughout the novel that this is the curse of much of the Buendía family, whose intensity of emotion and inwardness cannot accommodate social interaction. Those family members who are not solitary and hermetic, of course—like Aureliano Segundo—are radical extroverts. One of the complexities of *One Hundred Years of Solitude* is that even as the narrator treats the story very seriously and realistically, he also points out morals in the narrative, sometimes treating it like a fable.

What is suggested in the fable of the solitary Buendías is perhaps that human society is fundamentally polarizing and perhaps ultimately unfulfilling. Man is uncomfortable in society, and—as Aureliano and then José Arcadio Segundo discover—when he is alone, he may find comfort, but no great joy.

The reference in Chapter 4 to Big Mama's funeral, which will happen more than a hundred years after Melquíades is buried, reflects another aspect of Márquez's body of work: its intertextuality and web of connections among many of his short stories and novels. Though only touched on in *One Hundred Years of Solitude*, this funeral is the subject of a short story by García Márquez entitled "Big Mama's Funeral." Although it was published in 1962, five years before *One Hundred Years of Solitude*, "Big Mama's Funeral" mentions Colonel Aureliano Buendía and his war. Macondo is also mentioned in a number of other García Márquez stories, including his early work, *Leaf Storm*. These crossovers give García Márquez's body of work an almost mythical status; he has created not just a fiction, but a mythology of place and history.

CHAPTERS 5–6

SUMMARY: CHAPTER 5

Soon after Remedios reaches puberty, she and Aureliano are married. (Rebeca's wedding, which is to take place at the same time, is postponed because Pietro Crespi is called away by an urgent letter that says his mother is gravely ill. The letter proves false, and Amaranta is suspected of forging it to delay the marriage.) Remedios provides a breath of fresh air in the Buendía household, endearing herself to everybody and even deciding to raise Aureliano's bastard son—born to Pilar Ternera—as her own child. He is named Aureliano José. Soon after the marriage, however, Remedios dies of a sudden internal ailment, possibly a miscarriage, and the house plunges into mourning. This period of grief proves yet another in the interminable set of obstacles for Rebeca and Pietro Crespi, who cannot be married while the Buendía household is in mourning. Another setback is the tremendously long time it takes to build the first church in Macondo, which has been visited for the first time by organized religion. The priest who is building the church makes the startling discovery that José Arcadio Buendía's apparent madness is not as severe as everyone thinks. The gibberish he spouts is not nonsense, but pure Latin in which he can converse.

The period of mourning and delay are simultaneously brought to an end by the return of José Arcadio, the oldest son of José Arcadio Buendía. He is a beast of a man—enormously strong, tattooed all over his body, impulsive, and crude. Despite her engagement to Pietro Crespi, Rebeca is enthralled by José Arcadio's masculinity, and they begin a torrid affair, governed by lust. The affair ends in marriage, and they are exiled from the house by the outraged Ursula. There develops, however, a growing tenderness between Crespi and Amaranta, whom he had previously spurned in favor of Rebeca.

Aureliano, who had resigned himself to solitude after the death of Remedios, soon finds a larger concern: the impending war between the Conservative government—represented in Macondo by the magistrate who is Aureliano's father-in-law, Don Apolinar Moscote—and the insurgent Liberals. Upset by the dishonesty and corruption of the Conservatives, Aureliano allies himself with the Liberals. When war breaks out and the town is brutally occupied by the Conservative army, Aureliano leads young men of the town in a rebellion, conquering the town for the Liberals. He leaves at the head of a small Liberal army and is henceforth known in the novel as Colonel Aureliano Buendía. Eventually, he becomes the leader of the Liberal armies.

Summary: Chapter 6

Colonel Aureliano Buendía leaves Macondo with his hastily assembled troops and joins the national civil war effort, fathering seventeen children around the country as he goes. He leaves Arcadio—the illegitimate son of José Arcadio and Pilar Ternera—in charge of the town in his absence, and Arcadio becomes a dictator, obsessed with order and given to cruelty. When he tries to sleep with Pilar Ternera, his own mother, she sends him a young virgin named Santa Sofía de la Piedad instead. He marries her, and she gives birth to three children: Remedios the Beauty, Aureliano Segundo, and José Arcadio Segundo. When the Liberals lose the war and the Conservatives retake the town, Arcadio is executed by a firing squad. While the war rages, and Arcadio's dictatorship continues, Pietro Crespi proposes marriage to Amaranta, who cruelly rejects him despite her love for him, and he commits suicide. Penitent, she burns her hand horribly, covering it with the black bandage that she will wear until her death.

ANALYSIS: CHAPTERS 5–6

One Hundred Years of Solitude is remarkable for its scope: it is concerned both with events on a grand scale—such as the rebel uprising that begins in this section—and with the minute aspects of its protagonists' lives. It also runs the gamut from the sublime to the disgusting. In one breath, it seems, García Márquez will celebrate the supernatural, and in the next, he will investigate, in great detail, the filthiest of whorehouses. When, in this section, Remedios Moscote reaches puberty, it does not suffice for García Márquez to simply retell the fact: he also produces bloody proof. *One Hundred Years of Solitude* is a novel that, like the prophecies of Melquíades the gypsy, contains everything—the grand and the insignificant, the absurd and the transcendent. In that sense, *One Hundred Years of Solitude* is mimetic: that is, it imitates real life. Real life, of course, includes a seemingly infinite number of voices and a wide array of emotions and qualities. *One Hundred Years of Solitude* gets its epic scope from its attempt to imitate reality, to include everything that life includes. In *One Hundred Years of Solitude*'s attempt at mimesis, too, lies one reason for its confused timeline and tendency to jump from story to story without obvious transition. García Márquez believes that modern life is entropic—chaotic, tending toward eventual dissolution. Thus, he refuses to impose a rigid structure on his novel, choosing instead to allow the novel to meander digressively, at times unraveling, toward the eventual apocalypse at its close.

Despite García Márquez's determination to capture the variety and scope of real life, however, the reader will notice that his language sometimes tends toward the metaphoric and euphemistic rather than the literal and precise. For instance: although García Márquez does not shy away from a narration of the moment when Remedios Moscote first finds menstrual blood in her underwear, he avoids an actual mention of the blood. Instead, he calls it "chocolate-colored paste." And in describing Rebeca's first sex act with José Arcadio, García Márquez refers to her loss of virginity as a loss of "intimacy," a curious circumlocution. These moments leave us asking why García Márquez avoids graphic and realistic use of language throughout the novel in his descriptions of sex and violence and why a novel that explores all aspects of life, both beautiful and disgusting, substitutes euphemisms for a realistic depiction of events. One answer is that García Márquez brings the ordinary world into the realm of the fantastic by using poetic language for mundane things and mundane language for magical events.

Another answer might be that García Márquez is attempting, through these circumlocutions, to use language that his characters themselves might use. The novel speaks in Remedios Moscote's voice, describing her blood as she might have. This narrative technique, in which the novel assumes the voice of a character without openly indicating that it is switching perspectives, is known as free indirect discourse. *One Hundred Years of Solitude*'s epic feel can be accounted for by its multiplicity of voices, its desire to see things from different perspectives, and its descriptions of them in the subjective terms used by different characters.

It is not just the technological forces of modernization that cause the unraveling of Macondo's utopian, Eden-like community, but the arrival of organized religion in the form of priests and magistrates. Before the priest's arrival, shame is unknown in Macondo—like Adam and Eve before the fall, the citizens are "subject to the natural law" sexually and worship God without a church. Father Nicanor's arrival disturbs that untouched innocence, just as Don Apolinar Moscote's increased power (as he finally succeeds in bringing armed soldiers to help govern Macondo) disturbs the self-governing peace that the town has always enjoyed. Once Macondo's innocence has been lost, efforts to regain it by overthrowing the new leaders only make things worse. For example, Arcadio's revolution against Don Apolinar Moscote's regime only results in worse dictatorship. And, in addition to showing how impossible it is for the town to regain its innocence, Arcadio's dictatorship also shows what can go wrong when well-intentioned governments have cruel leaders and become power-obsessed. This commentary applies outside of the fictional world of *One Hundred Years of Solitude*, criticizing dictatorial regimes in twentieth-century Latin American countries like Cuba and Panama.

CHAPTERS 7–9

SUMMARY: CHAPTER 7

The Liberals have lost the war, and Colonel Aureliano Buendía, along with his friend Colonel Gerineldo Márquez, is captured and sentenced to execution by firing squad. His last request is that the sentence be carried out in his hometown of Macondo. He is saved at the final instant, however, by his brother José Arcadio, and, immediately, Colonel Buendía launches another uprising, one of thirty-two he will lead during his military career. He encounters a long string of failures, however, and is abandoned by the Liberal party's official representatives. Eventually, though, he enjoys some success and is able to recapture Macondo and other coastal territory. But an assassination attempt leaves him disillusioned with the constant fighting, and he begins to realize that he is fighting not for ideology but for pride alone. He starts writing poetry again, as he used to do during his courtship with Remedios Moscote.

While Aureliano is fighting his wars, Santa Sofía de la Piedad gives birth to twins fathered by her dead husband, Arcadio; they are named José Arcadio Segundo and Aureliano Segundo. Apart from this happy event, however, tragedy strikes the Buendía family repeatedly. José Arcadio dies mysteriously, and it is unclear whether he has been murdered or has committed suicide. Rebeca, his wife, becomes a hermit, living the rest of her life in solitary grief. Colonel Gerineldo Márquez, who is left in command of the town when Aureliano leaves yet again to fight, has been in love for years with the solitary Amaranta, who spurns him as she did Pietro Crespi. And finally, after years of living outside tied to a tree, José Arcadio Buendía, the patriarch of the clan, dies. A rain of yellow flowers from the sky marks his death.

SUMMARY: CHAPTER 8

> *Aureliano José had been destined to find . . . happiness . . . but had been directed by a wrong interpretation of the cards.* (See QUOTATIONS, p. 56)

Time passes, and Aureliano José, the son of Colonel Aureliano Buendía and Pilar Ternera, grows to maturity. He develops an unhealthy passion for his aunt, Amaranta, which she—in her loneliness—comes dangerously close to requiting. The two touch each other and sleep naked together without ever having intercourse. When they are almost discovered kissing, however, Amaranta breaks off the affair, and Aureliano José joins the army. The official Liberal party signs a peace agreement with the Conservative government, an agreement that Colonel Buendía sees as treacherous. He repudiates the agreement and flees the country, and Aureliano José goes with him. While Colonel Aureliano is traveling throughout the Caribbean, starting Liberal uprisings, Macondo settles into relative peace, thriving in its new status as a municipality under the mayor José Raquél Moncada, who is a Conservative but also a humane and intelligent man.

Aureliano José deserts the rebel army and returns home, hoping to marry Amaranta, who continues to avoid him, repelled by the notion of incest. The situation is brought to a tragic close when Aureliano José is killed by a Conservative soldier during an act of civil disobedience. Soon after Aureliano José's desertion, the seventeen sons whom Colonel Aureliano Buendía has fathered over the course of his travels are brought to Macondo to be baptized, and all are given the name Aureliano. Not long after Aureliano José's death, the Colonel himself returns to Macondo as the head of an army. Tall and pale, Colonel Aureliano Buendía has been hardened by his many battles: when a court martial orders that José Raquél Moncada be put to death, he refuses to commute the sentence, despite the longstanding friendship between the two soldiers and the protests of all the town's matriarchs.

SUMMARY: CHAPTER 9

The execution of Moncada is the beginning of the end. Colonel Gerineldo Márquez, and then Colonel Aureliano Buendía himself, lose faith in the purpose of the war. Gerineldo Márquez devotes himself instead to Amaranta, who steadily rebuffs his protestations of love even as she becomes more and more used to his presence. Withdrawn into himself, Colonel Buendía becomes a shell of a man, unemotional and utterly solitary, without any memories. It is only when Gerineldo Márquez is condemned to death that Colonel Buendía is forced to confront himself, finally acknowledging the emptiness of the war. Together with the freed Colonel Gerineldo Márquez, he fights the bloody battles against his own forces in an effort to convince the Liberals, at last, to end the war. When he signs a peace treaty that he feels represents the Liberal party's failure to uphold their ideals, he thinks that he has betrayed both himself and his party. He attempts suicide but survives the bullet wound in his chest. When Úrsula, his mother, sees that he will live, she makes an effort to rejuvenate the house and to rescue it from the creeping decay that descended on it during the war.

SUMMARY & ANALYSIS

ANALYSIS: CHAPTERS 7–9

This section, describing Colonel Aureliano Buendía's wars and the concurrent changes in Macondo, is one of the most disturbing in the novel. José Aureliano Buendía dies, and even the heavens mourn his passing, miraculously raining down yellow flowers in his memory. Death, in fact, begins to plague the Buendía family: José Arcadio,

Arcadio, and Aureliano José all die prematurely and tragically. But perhaps the most troubling of the misfortunes that fill these pages is the dehumanization of Colonel Aureliano Buendía. Once a sensitive man, the Colonel becomes hardened by war, losing his capacity for emotion and even for memory. In *One Hundred Years of Solitude*, miracles like the rain of flowers in honor of José Arcadio Buendía coexist with tragedies, and no mercy is shown to the protagonists.

Throughout *One Hundred Years of Solitude*, the possibility of forgetting the past threatens the coherence of society and relationships. Amnesia strikes Macondo early in the novel, and later, all memory of a massacre is eliminated. Colonel Aureliano Buendía's loss of memory is connected to his inability to experience emotion other than sadness and resignation. The cruel necessities of war have scourged him of any sensitivity and even of the tenderness associated with nostalgic longings for his past. His attempt to commit suicide is not so much a result of shame for having surrendered, one senses, but a way of eliminating his solitary sadness. In *One Hundred Years of Solitude*, emotion lodges in nostalgia and ties of affection spring from memories of the past. "How awful," Colonel Aureliano Buendía reflects when he returns home after the war, and he finds himself unmoved by seeing his family again and "the way time passes." The fears of change and of the accompanying dulling of emotion are augmented by the fear of memory loss, and Aureliano can barely remember what the past was like. Rebeca, on the other hand, lives her hermit's life accompanied only by memories, which walk "like human beings through the cloistered rooms" and bring her a peace that no actual humans have ever brought to her.

In this section, the novel expands to its largest scope, filled with the most characters; it contains the rebellion and other national political events. The novel seems noisy and crowded at this point, filled with a confusing multiplicity of voices and perspectives. But even as we are overwhelmed by these voices, the Buendías seem to be retreating further and further into solitude. We learn that a deep feeling of alienation lies at the core of Arcadio's obsession with order and his tyranny of the town when he is installed as dictator. Without the ability to connect emotionally with anybody, Colonel Aureliano Buendía retreats into the solitude of his empty mind. Rebeca shuts herself up in her house with memories that take the place of people, and Amaranta refuses all suitors despite her strong desire not to be alone. Úrsula Iguarán, having no one to confide in, talks only to her insane husband, who does not understand her because he now only speaks Latin. Language functions throughout the novel as a barrier between humans, a dilemma inspired by the biblical confusion of Babel.

Not only as individuals, but as a family, too, the Buendías begin to turn in upon themselves. Incest has been bubbling beneath the surface of the story all along: José Arcadio Buendía and Úrsula Iguarán are cousins, and Arcadio wants to sleep with Pilar Ternera, who is his mother. The urge for incest is now at full force as Aureliano José lusts after his lonely aunt, Amaranta, who is tempted by the young man but refuses to sleep with him, horrified by the taboo. This recurring urge, which will reappear again and again among the Buendías, is symptomatic, perhaps, of the family's alienation. They are isolated both in their remote town and by their solitary personalities. And it should be remembered that the act of incest is an essentially repetitive act: relatives who copulate are essentially reproducing and doubling family relationships that already exist. History, for the Buendía family, repeats itself in ever-tightening spirals, drawing the Buendía family inward upon themselves.

CHAPTERS 10–11

SUMMARY: CHAPTER 10
Colonel Aureliano Buendía has withdrawn even further from society, spending his days locked in his workshop making tiny golden fishes and refusing to speak about politics. Meanwhile, in his adolescence, Aureliano Segundo begins to delve into the esoteric mysteries still preserved in Melquíades's laboratory; he is often visited by the specter of Melquíades himself. José Arcadio Segundo—Aureliano Segundo's twin brother—on the other hand, begins to show a religious side. Soon, however, he becomes a cockfighter and sometimes engages in sex with donkeys. The two brothers, who share a strong resemblance until they are fully grown, both start sleeping with the same woman, Petra Cotes, who does not realize that they are not the same man. When Jose Arcadio Segundo is scared off by a venereal disease contracted from Petra Cotes, he ends all contact, while Aureliano Segundo decides to stay with her. The two have a fierce passion for each other, and something magical in their union causes their farm animals to be supernaturally fertile. Soon, Aureliano Segundo becomes fabulously wealthy by virtue of his livestock's productivity. He throws huge parties and engages in colossal displays of wealth. The whole village seems to share in his prosperity.

Driven, like his great-grandfather José Arcadio Buendía, by the impulse to explore, José Arcadio Segundo tries to engineer a navigable river passage to the ocean. He is successful only once in bringing a boat up the river. In his boat are a group of French prostitutes who promote a huge carnival in Macondo. Remedios the Beauty is declared queen of the carnival. She has become the most beautiful woman anyone has ever seen, but still she remains blissfully ignorant and totally innocent, like a child. At the carnival, however, disaster strikes. A rival queen, Fernanda del Carpio, arrives, escorted by mysterious men who begin a riot and then begin firing rifles into the crowd, killing many revelers.

SUMMARY: CHAPTER 11

The chapter begins by providing us with a history of Fernanda del Carpio. She is raised to believe she is destined for greatness, but her family's wealth has been fading, and her aristocratic line is dying. Upon seeing her at the carnival, Aureliano Segundo becomes obsessed with her, tracking her down in her gloomy city and carrying her home to marry him. Their personalities, however, clash: she is religious and haughty, while he is a devoted hedonist. Scorning his wife's rigid moral and social code, Aureliano Segundo continues to sleep with Petra Cotes, both to ensure the fertility of his animals and because of his wife's prudishness in bed. Meanwhile, Fernanda attempts to transform the once- relaxed Buendía house into a facsimile of her aristocratic home. She rules with an iron hand, and the house becomes rigidly formal and unpleasant. Despite their estrangement, Aureliano Segundo and Fernanda have two children early in their marriage: Renata Remedios (whom everyone calls Meme), and José Arcadio (II). Úrsula, the hundred-year-old matriarch of the clan, says that José Arcadio will become pope.

Soon after the birth of Meme, the anniversary of the armistice that ended the civil war occurs, and the president of the Republic tries to honor Colonel Aureliano Buendía with the Order of Merit, which he declines scornfully. His seventeen illegitimate sons, each named Aureliano, arrive at Macondo to celebrate the anniversary, and Aureliano Segundo greets their arrival with revelry, much to Fernanda's consternation. When the seventeen Aurelianos receive the cross of ashes on their foreheads on Ash Wednesday, they do not wash off, and all seventeen brothers keep the mark until their deaths. One of the sons, Aureliano Triste, discovers that Rebeca, the widow of José Arcadio Buendía's son José Arcadio, is still living as a hermit in her house. Aureliano Triste and another of the Aurelianos, Aureliano Centeno, decide to remain in Macondo and build an ice factory there, in a sense fulfilling José Arcadio Buendía's early prophecy of a town made of ice. Finally, funded by Aureliano Segundo, Aureliano Triste builds a railroad connection, decisively linking Macondo with the industrial, modern world.

ANALYSIS: CHAPTERS 10–11

Character traits are entirely hereditary in *One Hundred Years of Solitude*; characters are defined largely by how their parents or namesakes behaved. But it appears that the babies in these chapters have been switched at birth: José Arcadio Segundo does not have the size and impulsiveness of his namesake, and Aureliano Segundo is not thin and solitary like the elder man of the same name, Colonel Aureliano Buendía. Instead, José Arcadio Segundo is intense and solitary like the old Colonel, and Aureliano Segundo is given to debauchery and excess, like José Arcadio. With only the names reversed and with such a strong physical resemblance that they are often mistaken for each other, the twins combine the traits of the José Arcadios and the Aurelianos into a single mishmash of identity.

The family is caught in a series of repetitions, with names and personality traits passed down from generation to generation. This pattern, however, is not a cyclical one but, rather, one that has many different lines of progression occurring simultaneously. Indeed, the family never returns to the exact same point that it started from, but instead cycles through moments and situations that are both similar and different from what has gone before.

The village of Macondo, at this point in the book, is beginning its long decline from the blissful innocence of former years. The announcement of the arrival of the train at the end of this chapter shows the sudden clash between Macondo's old-fashioned simplicity and the modern world: the woman who sees the train first describes it as "a kitchen dragging a village behind it!" The modernity that the train introduces to the isolated town brings a period of growth that only serves to mask the decline of the true spirit of the town, the Buendía family. Úrsula Iguarán, whose common-sense wisdom so often proves correct in this novel, realizes it first: "The world is slowly coming to an end and those things [flying carpets and gypsy magic] don't happen here anymore." It is not that marvels do not come to Macondo; indeed, the technology brought by the train is far more miraculous than the magnets and telescopes that the gypsies used to bring. It is instead that the citizens of Macondo are losing their sense of the miraculous, the sense of dreamy wonderment that infused the first pages of *One Hundred Years of Solitude*.

While it is clear that the novel values exuberance and energy, in these chapters it becomes apparent that it rebels against the wielding of power and meaningless hierarchies. When Aureliano Segundo marries the beautiful-but-frigid Fernanda del Carpio, the novel seems to frown upon her attempts to infuse the Buendía household with false aristocratic pretensions and hollow religious values. Throughout is a skeptical look at the institution of organized religion. The characters whom the novel celebrates—especially Aureliano Segundo and José Arcadio Buendía—are not followers of organized Catholicism. José Arcadio Buendía mocks the local priest, and Aureliano Segundo keeps both a wife and a concubine and laughs at the idea of his son becoming pope. It is certainly implied that Macondo was a better place—with more freedom, lightheartedness, and spiritual integrity—before organized religion came to the city. This is not to say that *One Hundred Years of Solitude* is an anti-religious book. On the contrary, it places great stock in miracles and in faith. But the religion in *One Hundred Years of Solitude*, like the general moral and ethic value system of the book, rests lightly on its adherents. Religion is a matter, as the earliest inhabitants of the town tell the first priest who comes to Macondo, between man and God, free of intermediaries. *One Hundred Years of Solitude* suggests that life is best when lived with exuberance and with few inhibitions: certainly, most of the characters in the novel seem to be uninhibited by traditional religious morals, sexual or otherwise. Thus Fernanda del Carpio is made to seem foolish for her strict adherence to Catholic principles, while Petra Cotes, Aureliano Segundo's lascivious concubine, seems to be rewarded for her promiscuous behavior with fabulous wealth.

CHAPTERS 12–13

SUMMARY: CHAPTER 12

> *It was as if God had decided to put to the test every capacity for surprise....*   *(See* QUOTATIONS, *p. 57)*

The influx of modern technology that arrived in Macondo with the railroad is amazing and troubling to the citizens of the now-thriving village. But doubly confusing is the arrival in Macondo of foreign capitalists who establish a banana plantation in the village and set up their own fenced-in town right next to Macondo. Macondo rapidly becomes more cosmopolitan: the cinema, phonographs, luxury imports, and more and more prostitutes arrive in the town. It is a time of chaos and uncontrolled growth in Macondo, and Aureliano Segundo is overjoyed by the overflowing energy. The only person who remains unexcited is the ethereal Remedios the Beauty, who seems blissfully unaware of the changes going on around her. She is unaware, too, that her beauty is deadly and that men die for the sin of loving her. In fact, she remains unconcerned with love and with men throughout the novel and seems unworldly until one day she floats off the ground and up to heaven, disappearing forever.

With capitalism running rampant in Macondo, Colonel Aureliano Buendía begins to repent his decision to end the war against the Conservatives, who are facilitating the rise to power of the foreign imperialists. The wealthy banana plantation owners set up their own dictatorial police force, which brutally attacks citizens for even the slightest offenses. Colonel Buendía's threat to start a war, with his seventeen sons as soldiers, results in tragedy: unnamed assassins track the boys down and kill all but one of them, shooting them in the crosses that are indelibly marked, like targets, on their foreheads. Colonel Buendía falls into a deep depression and visits Colonel Gerineldo Márquez in an attempt to start another war, but Colonel Márquez rebuffs him.

SUMMARY: CHAPTER 13

Úrsula, meanwhile, has grown very old and notices that time is passing more quickly now than it did in the old days. She is going blind, but no one notices, because she always knows where everyone is according to his or her daily routine. Úrsula is driven by a dedication to José Arcadio II becoming pope. Nevertheless, she is deeply sad at all the tragedy that has befallen the family. When José Arcadio II goes away to seminary and Meme to school, the house becomes even emptier. Amaranta starts weaving her own shroud in preparation for death. Fernanda del Carpio gains increasing domestic control and tries again to impose her harsh, religious discipline on the household. As a result, Aureliano Segundo moves into the house of his concubine, Petra Cotes, carrying his revelry to new heights. On one occasion, he almost kills himself in an eating contest with a woman known as The Elephant. In the absence of the children, the house becomes grim and ghostly quiet. When Meme comes home from school, however, Aureliano Segundo comes home from Petra Cotes's to play the part of a father. When she brings home seventy-two guests from school one vacation, however, it becomes clear that she has inherited her father's propensity toward reckless abandon.

Eventually, the solitary and enigmatic José Arcadio Segundo reappears around the house to talk with the old Colonel. But the Colonel does not respond well and instead withdraws even further into himself. Incapable of deep emotion and longing for some concrete memories of his past, the solitary old man drifts further toward death. He stops making new fish out of gold, which is his one constant hobby, and instead makes only a few fish before melting them down to start all over again. Finally, one morning, he passes away.

ANALYSIS : CHAPTERS 12–13

There is a certain amount of irony in García Márquez's proposition that modern technology and the pace of modern change confuse the villagers' sense of reality. After all, these are people who seem unfazed by the plainly miraculous. This reversal of the reader's expectation is in fact a reversal of social norms: supernatural phenomena are expected in Macondo, but technological phenomena seem unreal. The reversal is especially apparent with the arrival of the train, which brings the confusion of modernity to Macondo: "It was as if God had decided to put to the test every capacity for surprise and was keeping the inhabitants of Macondo in a permanent alteration between excitement and disappointment, doubt and revelation, to such an extreme that no one knew for certain where the limits of reality lay." As *One Hundred Years of Solitude* progresses, technology takes the place of supernatural events: the engineers of the banana company are said to be "endowed with means that had been reserved for Divine Providence in former times."

There is also a real political and historical message behind this reversal of expectations. García Márquez is attempting to convey the extent of confusion that Western industrial technology created in the lives of Latin Americans, whose minds were comfortable with the mythic and the supernatural, but for whom an adjustment to modern culture was extremely difficult. The townspeople reject the cinema because technology here is the stuff of unreality and illusions, whereas the appearances of the ghosts of José Arcadio Buendía, or of Melquíades, are taken to be genuine phenomena. As readers of *One Hundred Years of Solitude,* we are expected to view both magic and technology as real, accepting that the difference between them is, at least in the novel, a question of perspective rather than objective fact.

The banana plantation later becomes the most tragic disturbance for the town because of the influx of new money and new inhabitants that it brings. The perfectly ordered village that José Arcadio Buendía founded becomes noisy and chaotic. Only Remedios the Beauty retains her sense of calm and her innocence. She is one of the most perplexing characters in the novel, because she seems to lack a personality of her own—she functions only as a symbol. Incapable of the deep introspection characteristic of the Buendías, Remedios the Beauty lacks a sense of self and an ability to empathize with others. She is driven only by animal emotions, and her only characteristics are innocence and heartbreaking beauty. She functions, then, not as a living person within the novel, but simply as a symbol of the beautiful innocence that Macondo has lost—an innocence similar to that of Adam and Eve before they ate the forbidden fruit and gained knowledge of nakedness and sin. Remedios the Beauty sees nakedness as the only natural way to walk around the house. In the tainted world of modern Macondo, corrupted by too much knowledge and technology, Remedios is a relic and a reminder of the past. It comes as a tragic realization that she is, in fact, too pure for the world, and she simply floats skyward and disappears, presumably summoned back into the heavens.

While Remedios the Beauty's untainted innocence seems reminiscent of the Garden of Eden, Úrsula's musings on time in Chapter 13 call to mind the Old Testament as a whole. She reflects that, in the old days, children grew up more slowly and time affected people more gently. This notion is similar to the early parts of the Bible, where people live for vast numbers of years; as the Bible moves on, it depicts time passing more quickly. García Márquez has used a similar technique to determine the pacing of *One Hundred Years of Solitude.* At first, the future stretches out limitlessly—people live without fear of death, and there is more than enough room in the world for all their children. As the book moves on, however, death plays a bigger role and time begins to pass so quickly that it becomes hard to keep up with. For instance, children grow into adults in the space of a chapter or two. In addition to paralleling the Bible, this increase in the pace of time reflects the span of a human life, where time seems limitless at first but starts to fly by as the years go on. In that sense, Macondo is like a human being, *One Hundred Years of Solitude,* its biography.

As time passes more quickly, the cycles of repetition that have been present throughout the novel happen on a smaller and smaller scale. Aureliano keeps on making gold fishes, but now he melts them down again and again and reworks them, closing himself up in that minute repetition. Blind Úrsula is able to function because she realizes that the people in the Buendía house repeat the same routines every day with no variation. And, just before Colonel Aureliano Buendía dies, he has a dream in which he realizes that he has dreamed the same dream every night for years. All these occurrences are symptoms of the spiral that winds around the Buendías, binding them in a web of the past that they cannot escape.

CHAPTERS 14–15

SUMMARY: CHAPTER 14

During the mourning period for Colonel Aureliano Buendía, Fernanda del Carpio gives birth to her third child with Aureliano Segundo, Amaranta Úrsula. For years, the elder Amaranta, who is the last living second-generation Buendía, has been retreating into her memories. Amaranta lives more in her lonely, regretful past than in the present. Visited with a premonition of her own death, she begins to sew her own funeral shroud. When she finishes, she announces to the whole town that she will die at dusk, and she offers to take with her letters from the living to the dead. Still a virgin, she dies. After Amaranta's death, Úrsula goes to her own bed and will not get up again for many years. She is often visited by little Amaranta Úrsula, with whom she develops a loving relationship.

Meme, the first daughter of Aureliano Segundo and Fernanda del Carpio, grows up as frivolous as her father, only feigning interest in the clavichord that her mother forces her to study. With her father, Meme develops a companionship based on shared interests and mutual distaste for Fernanda. She befriends a few American girls and starts to socialize with them, even learning a little English. Meme falls madly in love with Mauricio Babilonia, a mechanic working for the banana plantation who courts her bluntly and shamelessly and whose openness and solemnity entrance Meme. He is followed always by yellow butterflies. Fernanda discovers them kissing in a movie theater and confines the lovesick Meme to the house. When she deduces that Mauricio Babilonia sneaks into the house every night to make love to Meme, she posts a guard in the backyard. When Babilonia returns once more, the guard shoots him, shattering his spine and paralyzing him for the rest of his life.

SUMMARY: CHAPTER 15

The tragic paralysis of Mauricio Babilonia traumatizes Meme, striking her mute. Scandalized by Meme's behavior, Fernanda takes her on the long journey back to the city where Fernanda was born. Meme is interred in a convent, where she spends the rest of her life thinking about Mauricio Babilonia. Months after she arrives, one of the nuns from the convent appears at the Buendía house with Meme's illegitimate child, fathered by Mauricio Babilonia, whom Fernanda keeps hidden in Colonel Aureliano Buendía's old workshop. Ashamed of Meme's actions, she pretends that the child is a foundling. He bears the name of Aureliano (II).

Meanwhile, José Arcadio Segundo, the silent and solitary brother of Aureliano Segundo, has been organizing the banana plantation workers to strike in protest of the inhumane working conditions. Macondo is placed under martial law, and the workers respond by sabotaging the plantation. The government reacts by inviting more than 3,000 of the workers to gather for a meeting with the leadership of the province and to resolve their differences. The meeting is a trick, and the army surrounds the workers with machine guns and methodically kills them all. The corpses are collected onto a train and dumped into the sea. José Arcadio Segundo, taken for dead, is thrown onto the train as well, but he manages to jump off the train and walk back to Macondo. There, he is horrified to discover that all memory of the massacre has been wiped out—none of the people of Macondo remember what happened, and they refuse to believe José Arcadio Segundo when he tells them. A heavy, unrelenting rain falls on the town and does not stop, destroying any physical traces of the massacre.

The army and the government continue exterminating any surviving union leaders and denying all reports of a massacre. Finally, José Arcadio Segundo is tracked down at the Buendía house, where he is hiding in Melquíades' old room. Looking in the room, which seems to all the Buendías exactly as it was in the days of Melquíades, the soldiers see only decay, as if the room has aged immeasurably. They do not notice José Arcadio Segundo. Terrified of the outside world after the massacre, José Arcadio Segundo takes refuge in the gypsy's old room, studying Melquíades' incomprehensible manuscripts. Slowly, he becomes dead to the outside world and his obsession leads him to a loss of sanity. José Arcadio Segundo lives only for the study of his texts and to preserve the memory of the 3,000 who died in the massacre.

ANALYSIS: CHAPTERS 14–15

In addition to signaling the Buendía family's continuing spiral toward its eventual destruction, the dual tragedies of Meme's ruined love affair and the massacre of the striking banana workers allow the later generations of Buendías to revisit the events that shaped the lives of their ancestors. After Mauricio Babilonia is shot on Fernanda del Carpio's command, Meme is forced to become a nun in the same gloomy convent, in the same grim city, where her mother Fernanda lived. It is not difficult to see in Meme's return to Fernanda's birthplace an echo of the beginning, in which the child fulfils the grim destiny from which her mother was rescued by Aureliano Segundo's love. And in José Arcadio Segundo's allegiance with the strikers, too, lies a parallel—he has taken the place of Colonel Aureliano Buendía, who, in an earlier generation, fought for the rights of the working class. Later, after the massacre, he also inherits Colonel Aureliano's disillusionment with war and solitary nature, locking himself up with Melquíades's manuscripts, like the Colonel locked himself up with little fishes. With her typical wisdom, Úrsula Iguarán notices the generational similarities: "It's as if the world were repeating itself," she remarks.

The contrast between the harrowing nature of the workers' massacre and the frank manner in which it is told can be explained by García Márquez's use of personal recollections in the construction of his fictional plots. There is very little sensationalist talk about blood and gore. The machine gun fire is compared to a "whirlwind," and the crowd of workers to an "onion." The episode is over in a few pages, and it is almost immediately forgotten by everyone in town except José Arcadio Segundo. But García Márquez's matter-of-fact tone does nothing to lessen the horror of the incident. On the contrary, the massacre seems all the more brutal for the machine-like quality of its perpetrators and for the concise prose in which it is told, as if the author himself was too horrified to spend much time writing about the incident. This is not surprising, since the massacre was inspired by a horrific episode in García Márquez's own experience. As a child, García Márquez lived near a banana plantation, and, when the workers at the plantation went on strike, they were killed with machine guns and thrown into the ocean.

It is not only García Márquez's experiences and memories that are folded into the narrative but his political beliefs as well. In the story of Colonel Aureliano Buendía's fight for the Liberal party, it is impossible not to notice García Márquez's sympathy for the Liberals and their cause and his disdain for the corrupt Conservative government. These political parties, and the war between them, are not entirely fictional. Instead, the parties and the uprisings are fictionalized incarnations of the political struggles in García Márquez's native Colombia. Similarly, it is difficult to read García Márquez's chapters about the banana company in Macondo without recognizing that the underlying subtext is the history of Western imperialism in Latin America. In *One Hundred Years of Solitude*, García Márquez depicts the capitalist imperialism of the banana companies as voracious and harmful to the inhabitants of Macondo. Capitalism and imperialism, supported by the country's Conservative government, bring corruption and brutality to Macondo and oppression to the inhabitants. García Márquez is not simply writing fiction but is telling a story about politics and life in Latin America, speaking as the representative of an entire culture. *One Hundred Years of Solitude* is fiction that shoulders the burdens of social and cultural responsibility.

CHAPTERS 16–17

SUMMARY: CHAPTER 16

The rain that begins the night of the massacre does not stop for almost five years. Imprisoned by the rain, Aureliano Segundo lapses into a restful quiet, abandoning the debauchery of his earlier years. He begins to care for the children, Amaranta Úrsula and Aureliano (II), Meme's illegitimate son, who has finally escaped from the room where Fernanda del Carpio had been hiding him. Ursula, bed-ridden, grows more senile and less coherent, becoming merely a plaything for the children, who learn from her the stories of their ancestors. The rain eats away at the house and reduces Aureliano Segundo's vast fortune to nothing, as all the animals he bred with Petra Cotes die in the flooding. Fernanda occupies herself with contacting the telepathic doctors, who are trying to heal her from a disease of the uterus, and she also occupies herself by tormenting her husband, Aureliano Segundo, who loses his temper and breaks every valuable thing in the house. Aureliano Segundo, in turn, occupies himself with an attempt to find the fortune in gold coins that Úrsula has hidden somewhere in the backyard of the house. When the rains finally end, Macondo has suffered a precipitous decline. The banana plantations have been washed away, and the town is receding backward into memory.

SUMMARY: CHAPTER 17

With the end of the rains, Úrsula gets out of bed and tries to rehabilitate the Buendía house. She discovers José Arcadio Segundo, who has been sequestered in his room for years, trying to decipher the ancient prophecies of the gypsy Melquíades. Returning to the house of his concubine Petra Cotes and finding all their animals dead, they are forced to struggle as never before to make ends meet. Their parties are merely humble replicas of their old festivals of debauchery, but they are as happy as they have ever been, once again falling madly in love with each other. Aureliano Segundo finds himself spending less and less time with the children, who are swiftly aging. Aureliano (II) falls into the pattern of the family's tall, thin, solitary Aurelianos. Úrsula continues to regress into her past, eventually dying at more than 120 years old. Rebeca, José Arcadio's widow, also dies during this time.

A hellish heat wave descends on the town, and the townspeople begin to believe that they are plagued. Birds die in droves, and a strange, semi-human creature, the Wandering Jew, is discovered in the streets. The town assumes a broken-down, abandoned feel, and it fills up with nostalgia of its former prosperity. In the midst of this poverty, Aureliano Segundo devotes himself to raising the money to send Amaranta Úrsula to Europe for her education, but his great strength of former years has left him, and he is dying. José Arcadio Segundo, too, is living his last days, and he is finally making progress in deciphering Melquíades' prophecies and in initiating Aureliano (II) into both the pursuit of prophetic knowledge and the history of Macondo. Finally, Aureliano Segundo is able to send Amaranta Úrsula to Brussels. His task complete, he dies at the same instant as his twin brother José Arcadio Segundo, whose last words are a reminder to Aureliano (II) about the almost-forgotten massacre of the striking workers. In the confusion of the burial, Aureliano Segundo and José Arcadio Segundo's coffins are mixed up, and each is buried in the other's grave.

ANALYSIS: CHAPTERS 16–17

The nearly five-year flood that deluges Macondo, practically erasing all trace of the banana company from the land, parallels the Biblical flood that covered the earth in the time of Noah. Then, as in *One Hundred Years of Solitude,* the world had become full of wicked people, and in the Bible the cleansing flood obliterates them. And it is possible to read the years of rain in *One Hundred Years of Solitude* as ordained by God, in mourning for the massacred workers, and as a cleansing agent in Macondo. Another, more insidious possibility presents itself, however. We have already been told that the banana company has the capacity to bring rain, supplanting the Divine prowess of God Himself, and it is certainly implied that the replacement of God by modern technology is symptomatic of the shattered reality of Macondo. The novel hints that Mr. Brown of the banana company, the man who has replaced both God and the angel of death, has brought the rains in order to wash away all traces of the massacre and to erase memory.

With the death of José Arcadio Segundo at the end of this section, Aureliano (II) becomes the town's preserver of memories. As Aureliano (II) explores the town in the final pages of the book, he discovers that practically all its history has been forgotten: "the voracity of oblivion," García Márquez writes, "was undermining memories in a pitiless way." Úrsula Iguarán, who in her senility and extreme old age has become childlike, serves as a metaphor for the town. Shrunken in its old age and ignorant of its past, Macondo has returned almost to its infancy. As in the beginning of the town's history, gypsies come to town, and they bring the same technologies—magnets and magnifying glasses—that Melquíades once brought. "The town [is] so defeated and its inhabitants so removed from the rest of the world" that the gypsy gimmicks are once again the source of wonderment for the few inhabitants left in town. Ursula's statement that "time was not passing ... it was turning in a circle" is more and more accurate. Macondo, like the Buendía family, seems to be stuck in a series of circular repetitions, but it is also true that the town, and the family, are moving ever closer to their final end.

As Aureliano (II) begins to tell the story of what really happened to the banana workers, it is clear that his version of the story is quite different from the established one: "one would have thought that he was telling a hallucinated version, because it was radically opposed to the false one that historians had created and consecrated in their schoolbooks." Fictional history is seen as truth, while truth is seen as hallucination. This reversal mirrors the way in which García Márquez continues to shift the boundaries between reality and fantasy. In *One Hundred Years of Solitude*, accepted truth is sometimes less real than fantasy, and vice versa.

CHAPTERS 18–20

SUMMARY: CHAPTER 18

Aureliano (II) remains in Melquíades's old laboratory, visited occasionally by the ghost of the gypsy himself, who gives him clues and eventually helps him decipher the prophecies. Aureliano learns that the prophecies are written in Sanskrit and that they will be deciphered when they are one hundred years old. The Buendías have become poor, but they are supported by food sent to them by Aureliano Segundo's old concubine, Petra Cotes. Santa Sofía de la Piedad, the almost-invisible widow of Arcadio, finally gives up on the family, and, after a half-century of patiently tending to them, she simply walks away without any real indication of where she is going. Not long afterward, Fernanda del Carpio, who now does nothing but bemoan her fate and write to her children in Europe, dies, overcome with nostalgia.

A few months after Fernanda's death, her son José Arcadio (II) returns to Macondo. He has become a solitary, dissolute man. It turns out that he has not been studying in a seminary but has, rather, been counting on inheriting a large fortune. He is trapped in the old, dilapidated house, left with nothing but his memories and his delusions of grandeur. When he discovers the gold that Úrsula Iguarán hid under her bed, he falls into debauchery, sharing with the adolescent children of the town in long nights of revelry. In his loneliness, he begins to become friendly with the solitary Aureliano (II), who is making progress in his pursuit of knowledge. The two Buendías receive a visit from the last remaining son of Colonel Aureliano Buendía, who, like his sixteen brothers before him, is shot down by the police as he stands in front of the Buendía house. The developing relationship between Aureliano (II) and José Arcadio (II) is abruptly cut off when four of the children, with whom José Arcadio (II) once celebrated at a party, kill him in his bath and steal his gold.

SUMMARY: CHAPTER 19

Amaranta Úrsula returns to Macondo from Europe, bringing Gaston, her husband. He has followed her back to Macondo, even though he realizes that her love for her hometown is a nostalgic dream—energetic and determined, she wants to revitalize the house and the town, but Macondo's decline is irreversible. As Aureliano (II) wanders the rundown town, he discovers that almost no one remembers the Buendías, once the most notable family in the village. Following the family propensity toward incestuous love, Aureliano (II) falls in love with Amaranta Úrsula. He finds partial solace for his unrequited love in his newfound friendship with a wise Catalonian bookseller, and with four young scholars he meets in the bookstore. Together, the scholars prowl the underbelly of Macondo, visiting whorehouses and bars. In one brothel, Aureliano (II) is comforted by the ancient Pilar Ternera, his forgotten great-great-grandmother, who offers him her reliable wisdom and intuition. He also takes a lover, a black prostitute named Nigromanta. Gaston, bored in Macondo, becomes preoccupied with his dream of establishing an airmail service in Latin America. While Gaston is preoccupied, Aureliano (II) takes the opportunity to admit his love for Amaranta Úrsula. Eventually she yields, and they become lovers.

SUMMARY: CHAPTER 20

> [Aureliano] saw the epigraph of the parchments
> perfectly paced . . . in such a way that they coexisted in
> one instant.   (See QUOTATIONS, p. 58)

Gaston travels to Belgium to follow up on his business plans, and, when he learns of his wife's affair, he does not return. First, the Catalonian and then Aureliano (II)'s four scholar friends leave Macondo, a town now locked in its quiet death throes. In the midst of the solitude of Macondo, the love affair between Aureliano (II) and Amaranta Úrsula continues, fiercely and happily. The Buendía house falls into total disrepair, destroyed by the couple's rampant lovemaking and by the red ants that swarm everywhere. In fulfillment of the family matriarch Úrsula Iguarán's old fears about the dangers of incest, the lovers' baby, whom they also name Aureliano (III), is born with the tail of a pig. Amaranta Úrsula bleeds uncontrollably after giving birth and soon dies. Aureliano (II) seeks comfort in the arms of Nigromanta and in drink, but he forgets about the newborn baby. When he finds the corpse, ants are feeding on it. He realizes that the line of the Buendías has come to an end. He boards himself up in the house and is finally able to decipher Melquíades' ancient prophecies. They are a description of the entire history of the Buendía family, from the time of the founding of Macondo. As he reads, he finds that the text is at that very moment mirroring his own life, describing his act of reading as he reads. And around him, an apocalyptic wind swirls, ripping the town from its foundations, erasing it from memory.

*[Aureliano] had already understood that he would
never leave . . . races condemned to one hundred years of
solitude did not have a second opportunity on earth.
(See* QUOTATIONS, *p. 59)*

ANALYSIS: CHAPTERS 18–20

Suitably, the Buendía family spirals to its final demise with an act of incest: Aureliano (II) and Amaranta Úrsula, aunt and nephew, have a child, whom they predictably name Aureliano. They are the last two surviving members of the Buendía clan, and, like typical Buendías, they have clung to each other in solitude, isolated from the outside world. They are practically the last people remaining in Macondo, a town whose history has run its course and one that is destroyed in the final lines of the book by the wind of the apocalypse. One might get the sense that it is not only Macondo but the entire world that has been destroyed in that final Apocalyptic fury, and one would not be entirely wrong. In this novel, Macondo has become a world closed in upon itself: self-referential and encompassing the full scope of human emotion and human experience. Time has run out for the Buendía family, which, in some sense, has come to represent all of humanity, with the Adam and Eve figures of José Arcadio Buendía and Ursula Iguarán as its source. The suggestion is that humans, too, will have time run out on them when their endless cycles of repeating generations finally draw to a close. "[The] history of the family," García Márquez writes, "was a . . . turning wheel that would have gone on spinning into eternity were it not for the progressive and irremediable wearing of the axle."

Just as the incestuous relationship between Amaranta Úrsula and Aureliano (II) signals the inward collapse of the Buendía family tree, the reading of the prophecies signals time folding up on itself. As Aureliano (II) reads, past, present, and future all happen at once. In a sense, this has been happening throughout the book: ghosts from the past have appeared and disappeared, Pilar Ternera could read the future as well as the past, and the simultaneity through which the Buendías move has made the past, the present, and the future all identical. Aureliano (II)'s final moments are like a miniature version of what's been happening all along. Time, in *One Hundred Years of Solitude,* is not a single linear progression of unique events; instead, it is an infinite number of progressions happening simultaneously, in which no event can be considered unique because of its ties to both the past and the future, occurring at the same time somewhere else.

Melquíades' prophecies also occupy a peculiar place in time, since, although they are written as predictions for what will happen in the future, they are read by Aureliano (II) as an accurate history of the Buendía family. As the wind swirls around him, Aureliano (II) is finally able to decipher Melquíades' prophecies, and he finds that Melquíades has left behind a prophecy of the history of the town, which is accurate to the last detail. The text of the prophecy mirrors the reality of the town's history, so that Aureliano (II) is reading about his destruction as he experiences it. The sense of unavoidable destiny is strong: the Buendías, we realize, have long been living lives foretold—and thus, in a sense, ordained—by the all-knowing book. It might even be argued that the text of the prophecy, in fact, is identical to the book *One Hundred Years of Solitude,* and that Melquíades has served all along as a surrogate for the author, Gabriel García Márquez. Certainly the prophecy has succeeded as literature that simultaneously shapes and mirrors reality, just as *One Hundred Years of Solitude* tries to shape a fictional world while simultaneously mirroring the reality of García Márquez's Colombia. Melquíades's vision, early in the novel, of a city with walls of glass, has come true in a sense: Macondo is a city made of glass and of mirrors that reflect back the reality of the author's world.

IMPORTANT QUOTATIONS EXPLAINED

1. At that time Macondo was a village of twenty adobe houses, built on the bank of a river of clear water that ran along a bed of polished stones, which were white and enormous, like prehistoric eggs. The world was so recent that many things lacked names, and in order to indicate them it was necessary to point.

These lines come from the very first page of the novel. They establish Macondo as a kind of Eden, recalling the biblical tale of Adam naming the animals. This parallel to the Old Testament is present throughout the book, as Macondo slowly loses its innocence by seeking too much knowledge. At the same time, however, the reference to prehistoric eggs refers to an entirely different account of the origin of the world: evolution. By beginning the book with references to two entirely different accounts of creation, García Márquez tries to tell us that, in this book, he will invent his own mythology. It will not be based solely on the Bible, nor will it be totally grounded in science. Instead, it will ask us to accept several different myths at the same time.

2. Aureliano José had been destined to find with [Carmelita Montiel] the happiness that Amaranta had denied him, to have seven children, and to die in her arms of old age, but the bullet that entered his back and shattered his chest had been directed by a wrong interpretation of the cards.

Throughout *One Hundred Years of Solitude,* the idea of a predetermined fate is accepted as natural. Because time is cyclical, after all, seeing into the future can be as easy as remembering the past. In this passage from Chapter 8, however, a prediction not only foretells the future, but also actually affects it. The act of reading and interpreting has a magically powerful status in this novel. This power will be seen again in the last few pages of the book, where Aureliano (II)'s reading of the prophecies brings about the destruction of Macondo. In addition to assigning magical power to the fictional act of reading within the story, García Márquez also indicates his awareness of the importance of interpretation in any reading.

3.   It was as if God had decided to put to the test every capacity
      for surprise and was keeping the inhabitants of Macondo in
      a permanent alternation between excitement and
      disappointment, doubt and revelation, to such an extreme
      that no one knew for certain where the limits of reality lay. It
      was an intricate stew of truths and mirages that convulsed
      the ghost of José Arcadio Buendía with impatience and
      made him wander all through the house even in broad
      daylight.

This quote occurs just after the arrival of the railroad, when dozens
of new inventions—the phonograph, the telephone, the electric
lightbulb—have flooded Macondo. The citizens of Macondo, who
have accepted flying carpets and miraculous rains of yellow flowers
as part of the natural way of things, doubt the reality of technological inventions. This passage therefore represents a turning point for
Macondo. Whereas the citizens of Macondo once believed in the
magical and mythical world as their only reality, they must now
accept *both* science and magic. García Márquez makes use of humor
here, since one of the people who cannot believe in the telephone is the
ghost of José Arcadio Buendía, who is, himself, much more unbeliev-
able to modern eyes than any technological invention. But, in reading
One Hundred Years of Solitude, we are asked to abandon those modern eyes in favor of the perspective of those in Macondo. We must read
at all times with an awareness of both points of view.

QUOTATIONS

4. [Aureliano (II)] saw the epigraph of the parchments
    perfectly paced in the order of man's time and space: *The
    first of the line is tied to a tree and the last is being eaten by
    the ants. . . .* Melquíades had not put events in the order of a
    man's conventional time, but had concentrated a century of
    daily episodes in such a way that they coexisted in one
    instant.

In the final pages of *One Hundred Years of Solitude,* Aureliano (II)
deciphers the parchments and discovers that they collapse time so
that the entire history of Macondo occurs in a single instant.
Although García Márquez has written the novel in a mostly chronological fashion, there have been hints of this overlapping of time
throughout the book: ghosts from the past appear in the present; the
future takes its shape based on the actions of the past; amnesia
plunges the citizens of Macondo into a perpetual present with neither past nor future. In other words, time in Macondo has always
unfolded strangely. Only in this final moment do we find out that in
Macondo, there are two kinds of time: linear and cyclical. Both have
always existed simultaneously, and, even as the Buendías move forward along the straight line of time, they are also returning to the
beginning of time in an ever-shrinking spiral.

5. [Aureliano (II)] had already understood that he would never
leave that room, for it was foreseen that the city of mirrors
(or mirages) would be wiped out by the wind and exiled
from the memory of men at the precise moment when
Aureliano Babilonia would finish deciphering the
parchments, and that everything written on them was
unrepeatable since time immemorial and forever more,
because races condemned to one hundred years of solitude
did not have a second opportunity on earth.

As he reads Melquíades' writings in the final pages of the novel,
Aureliano (II) knows that he will never leave because the destruction
of his family is foretold in the prophecies; he believes absolutely in
the fate that those prophecies describe. This reference to fate has
caused a number of critics to think of *One Hundred Years of Solitude* as a pessimistic book because it seems to say that man has no
free will and that all actions are predetermined.

The description of Macondo as a city of "mirrors (or mirages)"
also provides a great deal of food for thought. In the final, prophetic
scene, mirrors have already been mentioned once, when Aureliano
reads about himself reading about himself and feels "as if he were
looking into a speaking mirror." A "city of mirrors," then, is a city
in which everything is reflected in writing. The written reflection of
Macondo exists not only in the prophecies, but also in *One Hundred Years of Solitude* itself. By coupling mirrors with mirages,
which are fictional images, García Márquez invites us to question
the reality of Macondo and forces us to be aware of our own act of
reading and imagining the story of the town.

This emphasis on reading and interpretation is also very important to this passage. Aureliano has just learned his father's name and
refers to himself for the first time as "Aureliano Babilonia." The reference to the tower of Babel emphasizes language and Aureliano's
role as a translator and interpreter of the prophecies. García
Márquez attaches supernatural power to the act of interpreting a
story, and he makes reading an action capable of destroying a town
and erasing memory. In doing so, he asks us, as readers, to be aware
of the power of interpretation and also to understand that the creation and destruction of Macondo have been entirely created by our
own act of reading.

QUOTATIONS

Key Facts

FULL TITLE
Cien Años de Soledad; One Hundred Years of Solitude

AUTHOR
Gabriel García Márquez

TYPE OF WORK
Novel

GENRE
Magical realism

LANGUAGE
Spanish

TIME AND PLACE WRITTEN
1965–1967, Mexico City

DATE OF FIRST PUBLICATION
1967

PUBLISHER
Editorial Sudamericanos, S.A.

NARRATOR
Omniscient and anonymous, but primarily concerned with what the Buendías are doing and how they are feeling.

POINT OF VIEW
Third person, but sometimes uses vivid descriptions to show the reader the world through the eyes of one of the characters.

TONE
Although García Márquez writes with wonder and is truly sympathetic to the deep emotions of his characters, he also maintains a certain detachment, so that we are always aware that the book is an account of Macondo as it appears to a modern, cultured eye.

TENSE
Past, with occasional flashbacks. There are also brief, single-sentence references to future events that unfold with the novel.

SETTING (TIME)
The early 1800s until the mid 1900s.

SETTING (PLACE)
Macondo, a fictional village in Colombia.

PROTAGONIST
The Buendía family; in a single character, Úrsula Iguarán, the soul and backbone of the family.

MAJOR CONFLICT
The struggle between old and new ways of life; tradition and modernity

RISING ACTION
Macondo's civil war; Macondo acquires a banana plantation.

CLIMAX
The banana workers go on strike and are massacred near the train station.

FALLING ACTION
The banana plantation shuts down; Macondo returns to its former isolation and backwardness; the Buendía clan dies out; Aureliano (II), who finally discovers how to read Melquíades's prophecies, realizes that the rise and fall of the Buendías has always been destined to happen

THEMES
The subjectivity of experienced reality; the inseparability of past, present, and future; the power of reading and of language

MOTIFS
Memory and forgetfulness; the Bible; the gypsies

SYMBOLS
Little gold fishes; the railroad; the English encyclopedia; the golden chamber pot

FORESHADOWING
The fact that both Colonel Aureliano Buendía and Arcadio will face firing squads is heavily foreshadowed in several places. The final, apocalyptic reading of the prophecies is also foreshadowed throughout the novel: García Márquez often mentions the prophecies in passing, and we see various members of the family puzzled by them at different times.

STUDY QUESTIONS & ESSAY TOPICS

STUDY QUESTIONS

1. *How might one argue that* ONE HUNDRED YEARS OF SOLITUDE *is a realistic novel, despite its fantastic and magical elements?*

One Hundred Years of Solitude shares many formal elements with traditional realist novels. García Márquez's novel does not shy away from depictions of violence and sex; it is concerned with, and directly addresses, complex political and social issues. The overall tone of the novel is matter-of-fact, with events portrayed bluntly, as if they actually occurred.

Even those elements in *One Hundred Years of Solitude* that seem "magical" or fantastic are representations of García Márquez's reality. García Márquez's novel describes the unique reality of a Latin America caught between modernity and pre-industrialism, torn by civil war, and ravaged by imperialism. In this environment, what might otherwise seem incredible begins to seem commonplace both to the novelist and to his readers. García Márquez's hometown witnessed a massacre much like the massacre of the workers in Macondo. In García Márquez's Latin America, real life, in its horror and beauty, begins to seem like a fantasy at once horrible and beautiful, and García Márquez's novel is an attempt to recreate and to capture that sense of real life. This is also a novel that grants myth—both biblical and indigenous Latin American—the same level of credibility as fact. It is sensitive to the magic that superstition and religion infuse into the world. *One Hundred Years of Solitude*, then, is a realistic novel in the sense that it asserts a unity between the surreal and the real: it asserts that magic is as real—as relevant, as present and as powerful—as what we normally take to be reality.

2. *What is the attitude of* ONE HUNDRED YEARS OF
SOLITUDE *toward modernity? What is its attitude
toward tradition?*

Modern technology and culture, along with the capitalism associated with them, often destabilize Macondo: the arrival of the train
reduces the town to chaos, and the banana company is one of the
few true forces of evil in the novel. Tradition in *One Hundred Years
of Solitude* is a source of comfort and wisdom and a source of the
novel's formal inspiration, as well: *One Hundred Years of Solitude*
owes a great deal to the indigenous Latin American folkloric and
mythological traditions. But the division between tradition and
modernity is not quite so simple. For instance, the moral codes
adopted by the novel's most respected characters are not traditional
codes but are, instead, far more progressive. Aureliano Segundo, for
instance, is rewarded for his extra-marital affair with Petra Cotes.
Traditional Catholicism is seen as repressive, while the novel's own
version of modern moral codes prevails.

3. *The famous critic Harold Bloom calls* ONE HUNDRED
   YEARS OF SOLITUDE *"The Bible of Macondo." To what
   extent is this true? To what extent does* ONE HUNDRED
   YEARS OF SOLITUDE *pattern itself after—or diverge
   from—the Bible?*

First of all, certain elements of *One Hundred Years of Solitude*'s plot
are extremely similar to that of the Bible. The novel opens with two
characters in an uncivilized area of the world, a world so new that
many things still have no names. The characters, like Adam and Eve,
establish a progeny that both populates the world and experiences
the world's gradual departure from a state of pristine beauty devoid
of pain or death. When the heinous massacre occurs, in which three
thousand people are killed, it rains for five years, cleansing the Earth
in water in much the same way that the biblical flood in the
time of Noah did. Finally, the book ends with an irreversible,
apocalyptic destruction.

   But beyond elements of the plot, stylistic qualities of the novel
make the book function in a way similar to the Bible. Not only has
the entire course of events been prophesied by Melquíades, but at
the end of the book, the distinction between Melquíades' prophesy
and the actual text, *One Hundred Years of Solitude* which we are
reading, is blurred. It is possible, then, that the novel is itself, like the
Bible, a book of prophesy. But the prophesies do not necessarily
function for the residents of Macondo as the Bible does for those
who read it. If the book is indeed identical with Melquíades' prophesies, because the prophesies are written in Sanskrit, those who
inhabit Macondo cannot turn to them for guidance or information
about the future. While the Bible has a long tradition of exegesis and
interpretation, *One Hundred Years of Solitude* is available only to
Aureliano, who finally deciphers it, and to us, the readers. As a result,
when compared to the prophesies of the Bible, the novel's prophesies
are silent and inaccessible to those who could most use them.

QUESTIONS & ESSAYS

Suggested Essay Topics

1. In what ways can ONE HUNDRED YEARS OF SOLITUDE be seen as a fable about the history of human civilization?

2. How does García Márquez use symbolism in ONE HUNDRED YEARS OF SOLITUDE? To what extent does the novel function as a network of symbols, allegories, and parables; to what extent can it stand on its own as a narrative?

3. ONE HUNDRED YEARS OF SOLITUDE is a vastly ambitious book, attempting to bridge many dualisms and appeal to many audiences: it is both general and particular, both realistic and magical. Is the book successful in its attempts to encompass such a vast scope of experiences and voices? What are the narrative shortcomings of ONE HUNDRED YEARS OF SOLITUDE?

4. With which character in ONE HUNDRED YEARS OF SOLITUDE do you most identify? Why? Is there any character in the novel who is wholly admirable, anyone who is wholly evil?

5. What do you think is the novel's understanding of human nature? Is it a fundamentally optimistic novel? To what extent does García Márquez believe that love is possible?

6. To what extent is the novel's title, ONE HUNDRED YEARS OF SOLITUDE, an important commentary on the narrative in the book? What connections does the book make between knowledge and solitude? Is solitude an unavoidable condition of human nature?

7. To what extent do you think that ONE HUNDRED YEARS OF SOLITUDE is a novel particularly concerned with Latin American culture and politics? To what extent is it a novel designed to appeal broadly to all readers?

REVIEW & RESOURCES

QUIZ

1. What is the name of the gypsy who brings the magnet and telescope to Macondo?

   A. Alfonso
   B. Riohacha
   C. Melquíades
   D. Teófilo Vargas

2. What is the nickname of the woman who beats Aureliano Segundo in an eating contest?

   A. Remedios
   B. The Elephant
   C. Petra Cotes
   D. Lourdes

3. When Colonel Aureliano Buendía retires from the war, what does he spend his time making?

   A. Golden fishes
   B. Ceramic pottery
   C. Lottery tickets
   D. Maps

4. What is the name of the man whom José Arcadio Buendía kills for making fun of him?

   A. Giovanni della Mirandola
   B. Mario Vargas Llosa
   C. El Guapo
   D. Prudencio Aguilar

5. After a certain point in the novel, what mark distinguishes Colonel Aureliano Buendía's seventeen sons?

    A. They are all extremely fat
    B. They all have golden eyes
    C. They all have crosses on their forehead
    D. They all wear only black clothing

6. What invention does Aureliano Triste bring to Macondo?

    A. The railroad
    B. The gyroscope
    C. The airplane
    D. Gunpowder

7. The civil war is fought between which two parties?

    A. The monarchists and the loyalists
    B. The Liberals and the Conservatives
    C. The Extremists and the Pacifists
    D. The Whigs and the Tories

8. According to Buendía family tradition, what will happen to babies born of incestuous relationships?

    A. They will be extremely small
    B. They will float away into the sky
    C. They will have wings like bats
    D. They will have tails like pigs

9. What happens to Remedios the Beauty?

    A. She is abducted by gypsies
    B. She floats away into the sky
    C. She marries the local bookseller
    D. She becomes a hermit

10. How does the government put Arcadio to death?

    A. Firing squad
    B. Hanging
    C. Electrocution
    D. Beheading

11. Aureliano (II) discovers that the prophecies are written in which language?

   A. Latin
   B. Hittite
   C. Ancient Greek
   D. Sanskrit

12. Which of the following best describes Dr. Alirio Noguera?

   A. Pediatrician
   B. Liberal radical
   C. Alchemist
   D. Fortune teller

13. Where is Úrsula Iguarán's gold hidden?

   A. Under her bed
   B. In the church
   C. Underneath the tree in the backyard
   D. In Colonel Aureliano Buendía's workshop

14. What job does Mauricio Babilonia do for the banana company?

   A. He is a foreman
   B. He is a security guard
   C. He is a mechanic
   D. He is a banana picker

15. What instrument does Pietro Crespi bring to the Buendía household?

   A. The harp
   B. The pianola
   C. The harpsichord
   D. The timpani

16. What is the name of the first magistrate to come to Macondo, whose daughter marries Colonel Aureliano Buendía?

    A.   Don Apolinar Moscote
    B.   Don Pedro Vasquez
    C.   Don Reymondo Ordoñez
    D.   Don Isaac Abravanel

17. As a mark of her regret, what does Amaranta wear until she dies?

    A.   A cross around her neck
    B.   A scarlet handkerchief over her hair
    C.   A black bandage on her hand
    D.   A crown of thorns around her forehead

18. Which bad habit does Rebeca not have when she first comes to Macondo?

    A.   Eating dirt
    B.   Eating whitewash
    C.   Sucking her finger
    D.   Bathing in mud

19. What is the name of the black woman who becomes Aureliano (II)'s lover?

    A.   Nigromanta
    B.   Cornelia
    C.   Claudia Arribata
    D.   Marcela

20. Gaston, Amaranta Úrsula's husband, tries to start which kind of business?

    A.   Selling books
    B.   Delivering airmail
    C.   Teaching music
    D.   Making ice

21. Jose Aureliano Segundo is the sole surviving witness to what catastrophe?

    A. The flood in town
    B. The great fire in the church
    C. The collapse of the Buendía house in an earthquake
    D. The massacre of the striking workers

22. How do Aureliano Segundo and Petra Cotes become rich?

    A. They find Úrsula Iguarán's buried gold
    B. Their farm animals breed extremely rapidly
    C. They are very successful selling the candy that they make
    D. They go to work at the banana plantation

23. Aureliano José is shot in the back while running away from soldiers in which building?

    A. The movie theater
    B. The church
    C. The brothel
    D. The Buendía house

24. What infectious disease does Rebeca bring to Macondo?

    A. Measles
    B. Insomnia
    C. Leprosy
    D. Smallpox

25. What do Aureliano (II) and Amaranta Úrsula name their baby?

    A. Aureliano
    B. Mauricio Babilonia
    C. José
    D. Gerineldo Marquez

REVIEW & RESOURCES

SUGGESTIONS FOR FURTHER READING

BELL, MICHAEL. *Gabriel García Márquez: Solitude and Solidarity.* United Kingdom: Macmillan, 1993.

BLOOM, HAROLD, ed. *Modern Critical Views: Gabriel García Márquez.* New York: Chelsea House Publishers, 1989.

"Gabriel García Márquez." From the Internet Public Library. *http://www.ipl.org/cgi-bin/ref/litcrit/litcrit.out.pl?au=gar-273*

GARCÍA MÁRQUEZ, GABRIEL. *One Hundred Years of Solitude.* Trans. Gregory Rabassa. New York: Harper & Row, 1970.

JANES, REGINA. ONE HUNDRED YEARS OF SOLITUDE: *Modes of Reading.* Boston: Twayne Publishers, 1991.

MCGUIRK, BERNARD and RICHARD CARDWELL, eds. *Gabriel García Márquez: New Readings.* New York: Cambridge University Press, 1987.

MCMURRAY, GEORGE R., ed. *Critical Essays on Gabriel García Márquez.* Boston: G.K. Hall, 1987.

REVIEW & RESOURCES

SPARKNOTES
TEST PREPARATION
GUIDES

The SparkNotes team figured it was time to cut standardized tests down to size. We've studied the tests for you, so that SparkNotes test prep guides are:

Smarter:
Packed with critical-thinking skills and test-
taking strategies that will improve your score.

Better:
Fully up to date, covering all new features of the tests,
with study tips on every type of question.

Faster:
Our books cover exactly what you need to
know for the test. No more, no less.

SparkNotes Guide to the SAT & PSAT
SparkNotes Guide to the SAT & PSAT — Deluxe Internet Edition
SparkNotes Guide to the ACT
SparkNotes Guide to the ACT — Deluxe Internet Edition
SparkNotes Guide to the SAT II Writing
SparkNotes Guide to the SAT II U.S. History
SparkNotes Guide to the SAT II Math Ic
SparkNotes Guide to the SAT II Math IIc
SparkNotes Guide to the SAT II Biology
SparkNotes Guide to the SAT II Physics

Spark Notes Literature Guides